John's Letters

How to Grow in Loving God

Written by
Daniel Akin

Adult January Bible Study 2007
LifeWay Press®
Nashville, TN

ISBN: 1-4158-3227-7

This book is a resource in the Leadership and Skill Development category
of the Christian Growth Study Plan.
Course CG-1176

Subject Area: Bible Studies
Dewey Decimal Classification Number: 227.9
Subject Heading: BIBLE. N.T. JOHN \ EPISTLES \ STUDY

Printed in the United States of America

Leadership and Adult Publishing
LifeWay Church Resources
One LifeWay Plaza
Nashville, TN 37234-0175

We believe the Bible has God for its author; salvation for its end; and truth, without any mixture of error, for its matter and that all Scripture is totally true and trustworthy. The 2000 statement of *The Baptist Faith and Message* is our doctrinal guideline.

Cover Image: Corbis

Contents

Session 1
Growing in Fellowship (1 John 1:1–2:14)

Session 2
Growing in Commitment (1 John 2:15–3:10)

Session 3
Growing by Loving Others (1 John 3:11–4:21)

Session 4
Growing in Confidence (1 John 5:1-21; 2 John; 3 John)

From the Editor

Continual growth in the Christian life characterizes the child of God, as does resistance to the things that stagnate growth. **The Letters of John**—with their emphasis on the person and work of Jesus Christ, the marks of true Christian behavior, and the believer's assurance of God's love in Christ—provide numerous opportunities for believers to learn to grow in their love for God.

This **Learner Guide** for **January Bible Study 2007** is written in an informal, easy-to-read style that helps the reader understand the biblical text without extensive comments. It also has a series of helps to enhance each reader's study. These helps include:

- Two **learning activities** in each chapter. Each activity is integral to the teaching plans in the Leader Guide.
- A least one feature entitled **A Closer Look** in each chapter that elaborates on or provides summary information on related chapter topics.
- Sets of questions in each chapter entitled **For Your Consideration** occur throughout each chapter. Some questions relate to Bible content. Some questions are application questions that help learners focus on the passage's present-day meaning for their lives. These questions can be used in individual or group study and with the Learning Activities can help a group leader stimulate discussion.

At the beginning of each lesson will will find the **Bible Truth** and **Life Impact.** The **Bible Truth** briefly states the main abiding spiritual principle for that lesson. The **Life Impact** identifies how learners will give evidence of spiritual transformation on an ongoing basis, so this is the main application we hope learners will take with them after the session is over.

Leaders will find further commentary (Expository Notes) and a guide for teaching (Teaching Plans) in the Adult Leader Guide (ISBN: 1-4158-3220-X).

Dr. Daniel Akin, president of Southeastern Baptist Theological Seminary in Wake Forest, North Carolina, wrote this Learner Guide.

CHAPTER ONE

Walk in the Light

BIBLE TRUTH: *An intimate relationship with God through Jesus Christ results in true moral living.*

LIFE IMPACT: *To help you develop intimacy with God through Jesus Christ*

Introduction To 1 John

Christianity stands or falls on the person and work of Jesus Christ. The options as to *who* He was and *what* He did basically can be reduced to four:

Liar – He was not who He said He was, and He knew it.

Lunatic – He was not who He thought He was and did not know it.

Legend – He was not who others later imagined Him to be.

Lord – He was who He said He was, and His life, death, and resurrection proves it to be so.

There's good news in that interest in Jesus is at an all time high. Back in July 1997, missions researcher David Barrett reported that 65,571 books had been written world wide about Jesus, with an average of four new books coming out every single day. Based on this data, there are today roughly 75,000 books about Jesus. Yet this "global explosion" in books about Jesus has not resulted in a more accurate understanding of Him. Rather, it appears there is greater confusion, misunderstanding, and inaccuracy than ever before.

We are confronted with inaccuracies, confusion, and blatant denial of Jesus in our day; but then, so was John in his day. In response, John began his first epistle to set the record straight about Jesus and to show us a life like no other.

The apostle John wrote five of our New Testament books. He wrote the Gospel of John to convert sinners, the epistles of John to confirm the saints, and the Revelation of John to coronate the Savior. To say it another way, he wrote the gospel for salvation (saved from sin's penalty), the epistles for sanctification (saved from sin's power), and the Revelation for glorification (saved from sin's presence).

Background to 1 John: The epistle of 1 John is a fascinating book. Written from Ephesus around A.D. 80-95 to churches in and around Ephesus (Asia Minor), it gives us four interpretive keys that help us unlock the five chapters and 105 verses of this letter:

> to promote true joy in the child of God—satisfaction (1:4);
> to prevent the child of God from sinning—sanctification (2:1);
> to protect the child of God from false teachers—safety (2:26); and
> to provide assurance of salvation for the child of God—security (5:13).

Themes in 1 John: Revolving around these four keys are the themes of belief in Jesus, obedience to God's commands, and love for one another. By these avenues, John provides tests for assurance of one's salvation.

Key Verse in 1 John: 1 John 5:13 serves as the overarching purpose statement, but not as the exclusive one: *I have written these things to you who believe in the name of the Son of God, so that you may know that you have eternal life.* It remarkably parallels the purpose statement of the Gospel of John (20:31).

Hence, the Gospel was written that we might *have* eternal life, but 1 John was written that we might *know* we have eternal life. It is possible to have it and not be certain of it, and John wants to clear that up. Belief, obedience, and love are an essential trio for clearing our minds and settling our hearts. So let's explore this helpful book written by a man who spent three years walking side by side with Jesus. John's intention for the letter was to assure its readers that their salvation was secure in the Lord Jesus.

In discussing his religious beliefs, Benjamin Franklin wrote:

"As to Jesus of Nazareth, my opinion of whom you particularly desire, I think the System of Morals and his Religion, as he left them to us, the best the World ever saw or is likely to see; but I apprehend it has received various corrupting Changes, and I have, with most of the present Dissenters in England, some Doubts as to his Divinity; *tho' it is a question I do not dogmatize upon having never studied it, and think it needless to busy myself with it now ...*" (Letter of Benjamin Franklin, March 9, 1790)

The first chapter of 1 John gives us reason why the person of Jesus Christ warrants us "busying" ourselves with studying Him. First, we see that Jesus is the Word of life, the only way to true life. Second, we see that Jesus offers fellowship with God to all who accept Him.

Jesus Is The Word of Life
(1 John 1:1-4)

First John begins in a similar way to that of Genesis and John's Gospel: "What was from the beginning." We learn three great truths about Jesus in these opening verses:

1. John encourages us to examine the Word of life (1:1-2). The "Word"—the fullness of God—was revealed in Jesus and was then "declared" by John and the apostles. Interestingly, the word "what" appears four times in verse 1, drawing attention to both the per-

Learning Activity
The Prologues of John

In your own words, describe in the space below the similarities of the two prologues.

John's Gospel (John 1:1-18)	1 John (1 John 1:1-4)

son of the Word (Jesus) and the proclamation of the Word (the gospel).

a. Christ is eternal in His deity (1:1). Jesus is fully God. He was before the beginning (John 8:58), in the beginning, from the beginning, and after the beginning. There never was a time when He was not. The Word of Life is co-eternal, co-existent, and co-equal with the Father.

b. Jesus is also historical in His humanity (1:1-2). The false teachers in the late 1st century denied His humanity and were, in a sense, the "New Agers" of the early Church (they're commonly referred to as "docetists" and "Gnostics"). They held that matter is evil and that salvation is attained by mystical knowledge.

These religious "know-it-alls" rejected the doctrine of the incarnation. Some said Jesus was a phantom who only *appeared* to have a body (John refuted them here in 1:1-4). Others said the mystical Christ-Spirit empowered Jesus at His baptism but left Him prior to His crucifixion (John will refute that in 5:6-12).

DesignPics

Why was John so convinced of Jesus' humanity? He gave four reasons:

First, the apostles heard Him with their ears (1:1). The disciples heard firsthand the actual words Jesus spoke.

Second, the apostles saw Him with their eyes (1:1-2). The word "saw" here is related to our word "theater." For three years John gazed upon Jesus. He watched His every move.

Third, the apostles touched Him with their hands (1:1). This is an unusual phrase, but it makes good sense against the backdrop of the Gnostic heresy. They physically touched Jesus and found Him to be real flesh and blood.

Fourth, the apostles declared Him with their mouths (1:2). God came down, and John heard Him, saw Him, touched Him, and now gave testimony to this "eternal life that was with the Father" (1:2). This is a testimony of personal experience. They were eyewitnesses.

It is absolutely essential that we get it right regarding Jesus. If we get this right, we'll be right in almost

A CLOSER LOOK

Light

The word "light" occurs 95 times in the New Testament alone. (See, for example, John 1:9; 8:12; 12:36,46.) First John 1:5 says "God is light, and there is absolutely no darkness in Him." John actually used a double negative in the Greek for emphasis. Read literally, it says, "darkness in Him not is none." This might be bad grammar for us today, but it's excellent theology. The term *light* conveys the idea of life and God as the source of life. John 1:4 reads, "Life was in Him, and that life was the light of men." Likewise, Jesus said in John 8:12, "I am the light of the world. Anyone who follows Me will never walk in the darkness but will have the light of life." Life is found only in Jesus. Denying Him is a rejection of the only One who can give life. Furthermore, it's a rejection of God and His character.

every other area of our theology. If we're wrong here, we'll be wrong elsewhere as well. "Busying" ourselves with Jesus is vital.

2. John encourages us to expound the Word of life (1:3). The main verb of the book's prologue is in verse 3: "we declare." John couldn't remain silent about this eternal, life-giving Word. Why is this so important? John said that Jesus offers people fellowship with God and a place in His family.

a. With Jesus you have fellowship. The term "fellowship" appears four times in John's writings (all in 1:3-7). The term implies something commonly shared among different people. Thus, fellowship with God is only possible by knowing Him—no fellowship, no eternal life. The two cannot be separated (1:3; 5:13). As a community (fellowship) of faith, we enjoy, as an aspect of eternal life, a relationship with the Father, His Son, and other believers. This is Christian fellowship.

b. With Jesus you have a family. God was known as a "father" only in a very limited sense in the Old Testament. Israel did not really address Him or know Him as "father." Indeed, to think of God as Father is totally foreign to almost all the religions of the world except Christianity. John learned to call God "Father" straight from the lips of Jesus. He is a Father who is good, gracious, and great. He is loving, kind, available, and approachable. Not only do you get a Father when you receive the Son as your Savior, you also get many brothers and sisters as well!

3. John encourages us to enjoy the Word of life (1:4). John's purpose for writing verses 1-3 was simple: "so that our joy may be complete." John was echoing here the words of Jesus:

John 15:11 – "I have spoken these things to you so that My joy may be in you and your joy may be complete."

John 16:24 – "Until now you have asked for nothing in My name. Ask and you will receive, that your joy may be complete."

The Westminster Shorter Catechism says, "The chief end of man is to glorify God and enjoy Him forever." What are some aspects of that joy we should experience?

We should enjoy our salvation (Ps. 51:12).

We should enjoy the scriptures (Jer. 15:16).

We should enjoy His strength (Neh. 8:10).

We should enjoy serving (Ps. 100:2).

We should enjoy the Spirit (Gal. 5:22; 1 Thess. 1:6).

We should enjoy soul-winning (Ps. 126:5).

We should enjoy suffering (Acts 5:41).

We should enjoy sharing (1 John 1:4).

For Your Consideration

1. Why did John write with such conviction regarding Jesus Christ?

A CLOSER LOOK

Advocate

The Greek word for "advocate" or "helper" is *paraclete*. It's used only five times in the entire New Testament—four times in reference to the Holy Spirit (John 14:16, 26; 15:26; 16:7) and this one time in 1 John 2:1 in reference to Jesus, giving us an advocate both in our heart and in heaven. A *paraclete* is "one called to help," one who comes alongside in time of need. This helper helps us when we sin. He is the Christ, God's Son, the Righteous one, *par excellence* (see. Is. 53:11, "my righteous servant," and Jer. 23:5-6). He is the cleanser of sin, forgiver of sin, the helper when we sin (Heb. 7:25).

2. According to verse 3, what does Jesus provide for the believer?

3. John greatly desired his readers to experience the indescribable joy found in a relationship with Jesus. What in your life is hindering you from experiencing the joy of salvation?

Jesus Provides Us Fellowship with God
(1 John 1:5–2:2)

Sin is an unpopular subject today, and great lengths are taken to hide, rationalize, or deny it. First John makes this much clear: in doing this, we *call God a liar*! It challenges His Word and questions His character.

John had an altogether different understanding both of sin's severity and a Savior's necessity. He recognized the separation between God and man caused by sin and the danger of calling God a liar.

Fellowship with God begins with one's relationship with the Lord Jesus Christ. To think correctly about Jesus, you must think correctly about sin. When you see sin for what it is, you will see your need for Jesus as your advocate (2:1) and your atonement (2:2). You'll not only avoid the error of calling God a liar, but you will enjoy the deep, intimate fellowship found in a right relationship with Jesus.

How can we avoid theological folly and enjoy fellowship with God? John gives us six directives:

1. Do not deny the character of God (1:5). Men call God a liar when they fail to understand who He is. John emphatically proclaimed that Jesus is perfect Light. He likely had in mind a passage like Psalm 27:1.

2. Do not deny the consequences of disobedience (1:6). John used three "if we say" statements (vv. 6,8,10). The first says: "If we say, 'We have fellowship with Him,' and walk in darkness, we are lying and are not practicing the truth." The "fellowship" discussed here is eternal life and is related to what we believe. If we believe what we say we do, we will "walk" accordingly. When the "talk" and the "walk" doesn't match up, we are speaking and living a lie, for it is by confession and conduct that we reveal whether we know God. As the great preacher, Charles Spurgeon, once said, "Sin may enter the heart [of a Christian] and fight

for dominion, but it cannot sit upon the throne. The Christian no longer loves sin. He looks upon it as a deadly serpent whose *very shadow* is to be avoided."

3. Do not deny the cure in the blood of Jesus (1:7). Verse 7 is the positive flip side to verse 6. John pointed out that Christ's blood provides both communion for the saints and cleansing from sin. To "walk in the light as He Himself is in the light" literally means to walk where He (God) is.

Interestingly, the Greek term for our English word "cleanse" is used in the present tense, indicating that Christ provides a continuous cleansing from "all" sin to all who walk in His light. Those who enjoy eternal life through Christ also enjoy a sinless status before God.

4. Do not deny the condition of all humanity (1:8-9). The second "If we say" is found in verse 8: "If we say, 'We have no sin,' we are deceiving ourselves, and the truth is not in us." In the previous verses, the lies were about their relationship with God; now they lie to themselves. As we learned before, if someone claims to be sinless, they claim no need for a Savior. Yet Romans 3:23 tells us that "*all* have sinned and fall short of the glory of God." Furthermore, Proverbs 28:13 says that "the one who conceals his sins will not prosper, but whoever confesses and renounces them will find mercy." To deny you that you are a sinner is to embrace falsehood; it is accepting a lie and walking in darkness.

To "walk" with God involves personal, continual, and confident confession of sin. How wonderful it is that God is both just and merciful. He is faithful to forgive—regardless of our sin. Our responsibility is to confess, repent, and put our faith in Jesus as our advocate and atonement.

5. Do not deny the correctness of God's Word (1:10). The third "if we say" passage is found here in verse 10: "If we say, 'We have not sinned,' we make Him a liar, and His word is not in us." First there is the tendency to lie to others (1:6). Then people lie to themselves (1:8). Now, they lie about God (1:10)! God has said that we're sinners; we arrogantly claim otherwise. God says, "You need a Savior," and we arrogantly deny it. There is a triple condemnation found here: (1) God is a liar; (2) I'm not a sinner; and (3) Jesus is not needed as a Savior.

Dostoyevsky was right in *The Brothers Karamazov*: "The one who lies to himself and believes his own lies comes to a point where he can distinguish no truth either within himself or around him, and thus enters into a state of disrespect towards himself and others. Respecting no one, he loves no one, and to amuse and divert himself in the absence of love, he gives himself up to his passions and his vulgar delights and becomes a complete animal in his vices, and all of it from lying to other people and himself."

6. *Do not deny the cost of salvation (2:1-2).* Today, fashionable theologians attempt to mold Jesus for their own uses—anywhere from a sandaled '60s hippie to a Marxist revolutionary. They're after a "feel good" Jesus. John is not interested in a Jesus with whom we are comfortable. John is interested in the Jesus who is real, the Jesus who is both our advocate and atonement.

a. Jesus is our Advocate: John wrote chapter 1 "so that you may not sin" (2:1). However, the implication in 2:1 is that we *will* sin: "But if anyone does sin..." John reaffirmed what his readers already knew—that "we have an advocate with the Father: Jesus Christ the righteous One." He is our advocate (our "helper") in our time of need.

b. Jesus is our atonement. He is our "propitiation" for sin. The word is also used in 1 John 4:10, Romans 3:25, and Hebrews 2:17, and means "satisfaction." 2 Corinthians 5:19 says, "in Christ, God was reconciling the world to Himself." Jesus, by His death, turned away the wrath of God from sinners. This teaches us that God takes sin very seriously. It also teaches us that His love for us is great. He is our advocate, our atonement. His *provision* is universal— for the whole world, but His *application* is limited—for those who acknowledge both their *sin* and their need for a *Savior*—a Savior who is Jesus Christ the righteous One.

For Your Consideration

1. After studying this lesson, translate into your own words the first part of 1:7: "But if we walk in the light as He Himself is in the light..." What are some ways in which you can "walk in the light"?

Learning Activity

Based on 1 John 2:1-2, choose the correct statement for each word listed below.

1. Koinonia
a. __ A coin operated laundromat
b. __ A small Greek restaurant
c. __ Fellowship, communion, or close relationship

2. Paraclete
a. __ A small bird usually kept in a cage
b. __ A pair of shoes worn when playing football
c. __ An advocate, one who comes along side and helps

3. Propitiation
a. __ The act of throwing a baseball by a major league pitcher
b. __ A change in the earth's atmosphere due to global warming
c. __ The removal of divine wrath through the blood of Jesus

2. What is Christian "fellowship"?

3. With whom do you have such fellowship?

4. First John 1:9 tells us, "If we confess our sins, He is faithful and righteous to forgive us our sins and to cleanse us from all unrighteousness." Many people have hidden sins which they think are hidden from everyone. However, nothing is hidden from God. Is there unconfessed sin in your life? If so, let go of that baggage to be "cleansed from all unrighteousness." God is faithful, and He will restore your fellowship with Him!

Obey His Commands

BIBLE TRUTH: *Those who obey Christ's commands give evidence that they have an intimate relationship with God.*

LIFE IMPACT: *To help you live obediently to Christ*

There are three questions in life that are important to every Christian, and all three might be answered by the same word. The three questions are: (1) What is the one true test that determines if your faith is real? (2) What is the one word that reveals whether you are merely a professor or genuine possessor of salvation? (3) What is the one thing that God desires most from His children? What is the one word that can answer all three questions? Obedience.

The essence of the Christian life is obedience. To love Christ is to obey Him. It can be argued as well that to know Him is to obey Him! So intimately wed are the ideas of love and knowledge that John used the word *love* 42 times in 1 John and the word *know* 45 times. We need to better understand a very significant concept: "Know and obey." This is not the *best* way to demonstrate our love for Jesus; it's the *only* way!

For John, there is a huge difference between saying and doing and saying and knowing. (For example, read 1:6,8,10 and 2:4,6,9.) In 2:3-14,

A CLOSER LOOK

"Walk just as He walked"

Scripture is clear that we should pattern our lives after Christ's life. Read these verses:

"Be imitators of me, as I also am of Christ" (1 Cor. 11:1).

"Therefore, be imitators of God, as dearly loved children" (Eph. 5:1).

"For you were called to this, because Christ also suffered for you, leaving you an example, so that you should follow in His steps" (1 Pet. 2:21).

Who do you pattern your life after? Do you want to be like the Father? Do you want to be like Jesus?

John pointed out that those who obey Christ's commands give evidence that they have an intimate relationship with God. Our obedience is a beautiful evidence of our salvation!

Profession Versus Proof
(1 John 2:3-6)

First John 2:3-6 says that obedience is the proof of the confidence we have in our salvation. John teaches us how we can be sure that we know the God who is light: through obedience to His commands. John tells us that there are four results to our obedience:

Through obedience we enjoy certainty (2:3). A brief, running commentary on verse 3 would go something like this: "This is how (*John was looking forward*) we are sure (*we can continually know with certainty*) that we have come to know Him: by keeping (*i.e. guarding as a precious treasure*) His commands."

After explaining the separation that sin causes between God and humanity ("walking in darkness"),

John described how we can know that we *know* God. We learned in Lesson 1 that Gnosticism was a false religion in the first century A.D. It was a heretical religion which argued that salvation was attained by mysterious knowledge. John, however, argued for a relational/spiritual knowledge that is personal, practical, and life-changing. The new birth—coming to Christ as advocate and atonement—places a new desire and passion in our hearts to keep his commands.

When the death and resurrection of Jesus establishes the new covenant (see Jer. 31:31-34), God writes His law upon the hearts of those who are His, and changes their hearts so that they will obey. Therefore, keeping the commandments is not a "condition" of knowing God, but rather a tell-tale "sign" that one does know God!

Through obedience we can escape hypocrisy (2:4). Remember the "if we say" sayings of chapter 1? Chapter 2 has its own; John repeated three times "The one who says" (vv. 4,6,9). The first "the one who says" is found here in verse 4: "The one who says, 'I have come to know Him,' without keeping His commands, is a liar, and the truth is not in him." This is the negative corollary to verse 3. To claim that you know someone intimately when you really don't is a complete fabrication—a lie.

How can we tell the truth-tellers from the "liars"? We can tell through obedience, of course. Disobedience exposes these sayers as liars and hypocrites. Truth is altogether absent from their life.

The tragic story of King Saul illustrates this. God gave Saul specific instructions for battle—to destroy everything, but 1 Samuel 15:9 tells us that Saul was not willing to obey. Rather, he only destroyed the *worthless* and *unwanted* things. God was rightly upset with Saul and removed him from the throne.

Obedience is doing God's work God's way. Obedience is doing what God wants you to do, when God wants you to do it, where God wants you to do it, the way God wants you to do it.

Through obedience, we can experience maturity (2:5). Verse 5 is set in contrast to verse 4 **but** takes John's argument a step forward by tying together the relationship of *knowing* God and *loving* God. It is a concise, yet faithful, summary of John 13–16 which emphasizes the connection between love and obedience. In stark contrast to the one who claims to know God but doesn't keep His commands (a "liar"), the person who keeps God's Word is indwelt by the truth, and the love of God has been completed in him. What a contrast between a *sayer* and a *keeper*!

Learning Activity
Obeying His Commands

On a scale of 1-10, with 1 being low and 10 being high, rate yourself as an obedient follower of Jesus Christ.

1. I seek to follow Christ through my actions on a daily basis.

1	2	3	4	5	6	7	8	9	10

2. I seek to follow Christ through my attitude on a daily basis.

1	2	3	4	5	6	7	8	9	10

3. I genuinely show Christ's love to all people at all times.

1	2	3	4	5	6	7	8	9	10

4. I am willing to make a bold stand for the gospel without fear of opposition.

1	2	3	4	5	6	7	8	9	10

5. When it comes to evidence of obeying Christ by my lifestyle, others would rate me as:

1	2	3	4	5	6	7	8	9	10

Why should a husband stay faithful to his wife and his marriage vows? Because he has to? Because he needs to? Actually, it should be because he wants to! He is constrained and compelled not by law, but by love. Fidelity to her does not make him love her. Rather, fidelity to her reveals and proves he loves her!

Through obedience, we can prove our confession

(2:6). Verse 6 is the second of the false teachers' claims to know God—a claim which, when rightly understood, can be made by a believer. The issue of becoming like Jesus now confronts us directly. As we've learned, it's one thing to *say* you know Him; it's something altogether different *to walk* like Him.

Verse 6 tells us that, as we proclaim our relationship with God, we should back up our talk with actions! Christians have a pattern to follow: "the one who says he remains in Him should walk *just as He walked.*"

Children love to imitate their parents. When I refereed basketball, my grandmother made little referee uniforms for my twin boys because they wanted to be like daddy! Like father, like son. Like Savior, like saint. Christ's life becomes your life, your pattern, your goal. The catch phrase "What Would Jesus Do?" is rooted in this verse.

For Your Consideration

1. In these verses, John described an essential trait that must be present in one's life to truly love God. What is that trait, and why is it impossible to love God without it?

2. First John 2:5 reads, "But whoever keeps His word, truly in him the love of God is perfected. This is how we know we are in Him." Describe in your own words what this verse means.

3. Is there a connection between "keeping His commands" (v. 3) and the concept of "fellowship" we read about in 1:3,6,7? Why is it impossible to have one without the other?

The New Command
(1 John 2:7-14)

First John 2:7 begins with a term of endearment used by John six times in this letter (2:7; 3:2,21; 4:1,7,11). It is the words, "Dear friends," and it begins a new thought. What John wrote is not new, but old, and focuses on "the commandment"—the commandment to love!

John said first that the love commandment is proclaimed in conversion (2:7). Much like today's culture, John's opponents minimized ethical behavior, saying, "how we live doesn't matter, it's what you know." John said, "not so." To love God is both to obey God and to serve your neighbor: "Do not take revenge or bear a grudge against members of your community, but love your neighbor as yourself; I am the Lord" (Lev. 19:18).

This old commandment is also seen in Christ (2:8). Verse 8 is not contradicting verse 7 here. John wants us to see how the "old command" takes on new meaning in Christ! The old is new in Him! Jesus said in John 13:34, "I give you a new commandment: love one another. Just as I have loved you, you must also love one another." In Christ, the love commandment is strengthened and given a depth of meaning and understanding it never knew before.

This command is also present in the Christian (2:8). It's "true in Him and in you." The love Christ has for us we can now have for others. John 13:35 adds, "By this all people will know that you are My disciples, if you have love for one another." This is a new, sacrificial, Christ-type of love, where we love others because that's how Jesus loves us.

Love is not new. Yet it is new to us in conversion and new in its depth in Jesus. It is new in experience, emphasis, expression, and endurance. It is old as the sun and new as the dawn.

Tradition says that when John was an old man at Ephesus, they brought him out on a pallet to speak to

the people. All he said was, "Love one another." When asked why, he simply replied, "It is enough." This was quite a change from the John who (1) was called a "Son of Thunder"; (2) wanted to forbid others from ministering in Jesus' name (Luke 9:49-50); (3) wanted to call down fire on a Samaritan village (Luke 9:51-56); and (4) fought over who would be first in God's Kingdom (Mark 10:35-45).

God did a great work in John's heart. He then understood how important it is that believers love another. Verses 9–11 each give ways in which loving others is important, especially for the believing community.

Love reflects our position (2:9). He who hates his brother (his neighbor, see Lev. 19:18)—and especially a fellow believer!—is not "in the light," but rather he positionally remains "in the darkness." He or she is lost—separated from the life of God. If you hate because of face, place, or race you are in darkness. You are lost and are unregenerate. There is no middle group, no in between position.

Love affects our practice (2:10). This is the flip side of 2:9. By loving your Christian brothers and sisters, you assure yourself that you won't "stumble" because you are walking as Christ walked. Not only will you personally not stumble, you won't cause others to stumble. A person who loves is not a curse to others, but a blessing.

Love affects our "perception" (2:11). This verse stands in contrast to verse 10 while reinforcing verse 9. When a person is filled with hate, he (1) is in darkness; (2) walks in darkness; (3) does not know where he is going; and (4) is blind. In the darkness, there is not only the absence of love, there is also the absence of God. The tragedy is that they don't even know it, having lived there so long.

Charles Finney once said, "Revival is nothing less than a new beginning of obedience to God.... When revival comes, obedience to the truth is the one thing that matters." He simply echoes Jesus' words in John 14:15, "If you love Me, you will keep My commandments."

But does God love everything? One day a little boy asked his mother, "Does God hate the devil?" Her response was probably what most would expect, "Honey, God doesn't hate anybody. He loves everyone and everything, and so should we." In reality, however, the mother's well intended answer was not altogether correct. The following verses reveal God hates evil, those who do evil, falsehood, lying, murder (see Ps. 5:5-6; 97:10; 119:104,113,163; Prov. 6:16-19; and Rev. 2:6).

To the verses above, I would add one other; interestingly, there is a particular *love* that God hates—*love for the world.* James 4:4 teaches us not even to make friends with the world. For in so doing, we become the enemy of God and 1 John 2:15 states "love for the Father is not in him."

First John 2:12-14 provides the encouragement necessary to observe the exhortation of verses 15-17: We belong to God. We're part of His family. He is our Father, and heaven is our home. With this knowledge, why would we give our affections to a world which stands in defiant opposition to our God?

God warns us that the world is seductive and deceptive. False teachers forsake the basic essentials of the Christian faith, no longer embracing the incarnation, rejecting the authority of Jesus' commands, believing they are sinless, and abandoning the idea of salvation through the work of Christ. They do not love one another. Righteous conduct for them is no longer a requirement of fellowship with God. Their loss of faith reveals that the love of the world has attacked and overcome their love for God. John wished to persuade them in 2:12-14 to abide in the love of God and to resist all temptations to love the world.

In these verses, John used three terms to identify his audience: (1) little children; (2) fathers; and (3) young men. Words of encouragement follow each address assuring them they belong to God and enjoy the blessings of that relationship.

John said that as little children, you are in the family (2:12,13c). "Little children" is a term of endearment which is addressed to all the members of the church "because your sins have been forgiven on account of His name." As children of God, they have confessed the name of Jesus; as a result of that confession, they now have two promises: forgiveness of sin and knowledge of God.

Although God is everyone's Creator, He is not everyone's Father. For God to be your Father, you must have His Son Jesus as your Savior.

John further said that as young men, you are in the fight (2:12b,14b). John moved from addressing the entire church to addressing young believers who were still growing in the faith. The phrase "young men" can refer to their age, their spiritual maturity, or both. Regardless, these young champions for Christ are engaged in the battle against Satan (vv. 13b,14b) and the evil system of the world (v. 15).

In this fight, John noted the certainty of victory in verses 13 and 14, as well as the weapon of their warfare. Their victory came the moment that they trusted in Jesus (1 John 5:5). In fact, the certainty of victory is repeated for emphasis. The outcome of the battle has already been determined, but we are still called to fight!

Finally, John said that as fathers, you are in the faith (2:13a,14a). This group of people consisted of the great warriors of the faith. They had walked with the Lord for many years, and their faith had been tried and proven. As "fathers," they had children (converts), and, being spiritually mature, they understood that "new" is not always better and "old" is not always   bad.
They had come to the conviction that the Jesus who saved them would sustain them. He was there from the beginning, and He would be there at the end. They had come to know Him, still know Him, and will always know Him.

For Your Consideration
1. In what way is John's command (v. 7) old and yet new?

2. Why is there such stress on love among believers?

3. How is love vital to Christian fellowship? How is it vital to our witness to the world?

A CLOSER LOOK
Spiritual Darkness

Those who hate their brothers live in a state of darkness where there is not just an absence of love, but an absence of God. Far from knowing God, those who hate their brothers and sisters walk around confused and lost, not knowing where they are going. Spiritual darkness is not a passive reality. It goes on the offensive. Darkness attacks those living in it so that they become increasingly trapped in this realm of confusion and blindness. In a real sense what we do is what we become. How we live is who we are. Habitual hatred leads to more hatred, and the possibility of loving becomes less and less likely.

4. First John 2:12 reads, "your sins have been forgiven on account of His name." How is Christ's name related to our forgiveness? (Refer to 1:9.)

5. "Hate" (2:9) can manifest itself in many different ways. Name some of them.

6. In what ways does your life mimic Christ's life of love?

7. What areas of your life demonstrate a form of "hatred" for others? How can this sin be corrected?

Learning Activity

Obedient Examples

1. List below the names of individuals you personally know who have been obedient examples of following Christ.

2. How have these individuals helped you in your spiritual journey?

3. How are you a better follower of Christ because of their examples?

CHAPTER THREE

Do Not Love the World

BIBLE TRUTH: *The world's value system entices people to sin, but believers stay committed to Christ as God shows them the truth.*

LIFE IMPACT: *To help you show your love for God by shunning worldly influences in your life*

The Disappearing of the World
(1 John 2:15-17)

More Americans than ever consider themselves nonreligious. A 2001 study found that 77% of Americans call themselves Christian (down from 86% in 1990). While Jesus still ranks among the top 10 most admired persons, only 69% believe He rose from the dead. Most people (71%) believe in heaven, while belief in hell plummets significantly to 53% of the population.

The world constantly beckons us to come over to its side. It tells us that you can think Jesus is important, but not preeminent. It tells us you can love God, and you can love the world.

John says not so. First John 2:15-17 moves from assurance to warning. Who you are will determine how you live, but how you live will give evi-

Learning Activity
Weapons of War

Read and compare the following Scripture passages. What similarities of weapons of seduction used by the world do you see in each passage? Record your responses below.

1. Genesis 3:6

2. Luke 4:1-13

3. 1 John 2:15-17

dence of whose you are. John gives us three things we need to know about the world in which we live:

1. We must know that the world is treacherous (2:15). Satan and his worldly enticements offer a fool's gold, a cotton candy diet, a paradise of indulging our carnal, fleshly desires. It is a system that seduces us, making sin look cool and righteousness intolerant. John cautions us to be careful! If you love this world, its things, its ways, "the love of the Father is not in you." Our allegiance must not be confused. Our devotion cannot be divided. Choose your lover, but choose carefully.

2. We must know that the world is tempting (2:16). First John 2:16 vividly identifies the weapons used by the world to seduce humans: the lust of the eyes, the lust of the flesh, and the pride of lifestyle. Interestingly, these are the same three weapons used against both Adam and Eve in the Garden (Gen. 3:6) and Jesus in the desert (Luke 4:1-13).

Look at Genesis 3: "The woman saw that the tree was good for food" (the lust of the flesh), "delightful to look at" (the lust of the eyes), and "desirable for obtaining wisdom" (the pride of lifestyle).

Compare this to Luke 4:3-11. "The devil said to Him … tell this stone to become bread" (lust of the flesh). Then the devil said, "I will give You [all the kingdoms of the world] and all this authority (lust of the eyes). Finally, the devil said, "If you are the Son of God, throw Yourself down [from the pinnacle of the temple]. For … He will give His angels orders concerning you" (the pride of lifestyle).

Take a closer look at each temptation: The lust of the flesh appeals to our appetites. "Lust" denotes a craving or strong desire. The object of our desire determines whether it is good or bad. Most often it's negative because its object is not the things of God.

"Flesh" may refer to the whole person, but here it conveys the tendency of humans to fulfill natural

A CLOSER LOOK

Pride

Jesus set an example regarding pride. In terms of human family, He was a carpenter's son, a poor man's child. Of possessions, He said, "The Son of man has no place to lay His head." Of pedigree, it was said, "Can anything good come out of Nazareth?" Of people he knew, it was said, "[He is] a friend of tax collectors and sinners." Of intellect, He said, "As the Father taught Me, I say these things." Of self-will, He said, "Father, if You are willing, take this cup away from Me—nevertheless, not My will, but Yours, be done." Of righteousness, it was said of Jesus, "God made him who had no sin to be sin for us, so that in him we might become the righteousness of God."

desires in a way contrary to God's will. Potentially, sexual appetite gives way to immorality, physical appetite gives way to gluttony, and sleep gives way to laziness.

We are not sinful because we sin. We sin because we are sinful. Let's not lie to ourselves: sin is enticing and attractive. We are drawn to it like a fly to a bug zapper.

The lust of our eyes appeals to our affections. Our eyes, like our natural desires, are not evil (Prov. 20:12). However, the eyes are windows to the mind (soul) by which sinful desires enter. This is why Jesus taught in Matthew 5:27-29 that the eye must be controlled. Males, being creatures of sight, must be especially on guard here. It was his eyes that led David to lie, commit adultery, and murder (2 Sam. 11).

The pride of lifestyle appeals to our ambitions. "Pride" is arrogance and refers to the braggart who exaggerates what he has in hopes of impressing others. It is the "I, me, my" person. "Pride of lifestyle" speaks of the person who glorifies himself rather than God. He or she makes an idol of their career, achievements, social standing, and possessions. Pride, power, possessions, prestige, and position are what lifestyle is all about.

3. We must know that the world is temporal (2:17). John concluded this section by contrasting two loves, two lives, and two approaches to life. We have to ask ourselves these questions: Why side with the world? Why give your life to an empty imitation, a worthless fake, a temporary illusion? The world, this evil, deceptive system of Satan's, *is continually passing away,* and its lust is going with it. What remains? What lasts? What endures? The answer: The one who *continually* does the will of God. Read what Jesus taught about the will of God in John 4:34; 5:30; 6:38; and 17:4.

The world loves us in order to abuse and destroy us. Jesus loves us in order to save and use us. The world's glory is for a moment, but God's glory is forever.

For Your Consideration

1. "If anyone loves the world, love for the Father is not in him" (1 John 2:15). Why is this the case?

2. What constitutes "lust of the flesh," "lust of the eyes," and "pride in one's lifestyle"? Examine each of these in light of your own life. Is there even a hint of any of them? If so, take a moment and seek God's forgiveness. Ask God for guidance in developing a plan of attack against such sin. How is this plan to be implemented?

3. We are told in 1 John 2:17 that this present world is passing away. Do you believe this—that all our worldly longings are worthless when compared to eternity? If so, how should Christians live in light of Christ's sacrifice? How does Titus 2:11-14 relate to your answer?

The Coming of the Antichrist
(1 John 2:18-27)

One important lesson we teach our children is how to tell time. With the creation of atomic clocks, our accuracy is precise, and with the invention of digital watches, our task has been made easier. Still, our time-conscious culture demands the ability to tell time—and tell it correctly.

John faced a similar challenge in the first century with respect to his spiritual children. However, John's task was even more important. The time that concerned him was not *chronological*, but *theological*; it was not time measured by man, but by God. According to God, it

A CLOSER LOOK

Antichrist

John is the only writer in the Bible to use the term *antichrist*. It appears only in 1 John 2:18,22; 4:3; 2 John 7. It is a word that John infuses with multiple but compatible meanings. "Antichrist" (Greek: *anti christos)* means "one who is against Christ" or "one seeking to replace Christ, a rival Christ, a counterfeit Christ." When reading 1 John 2:18 and 4:3, we learn that many antichrists (lowercase "a") have already come, and also that there is a spirit of antichrist that is presently operative in the world right now.

was—it is—the "last hour." John teaches us the clock is about to strike 12. The sand in the hourglass is almost gone. We know this because unmistakable evidence has appeared: the antichrists have come.

The word *antichrist* strikes a sense of wonder (even fear) in our hearts—and well it should! Given the wild speculation and outrageous ideas that surface about the term, it's essential that we have a correct, bib-

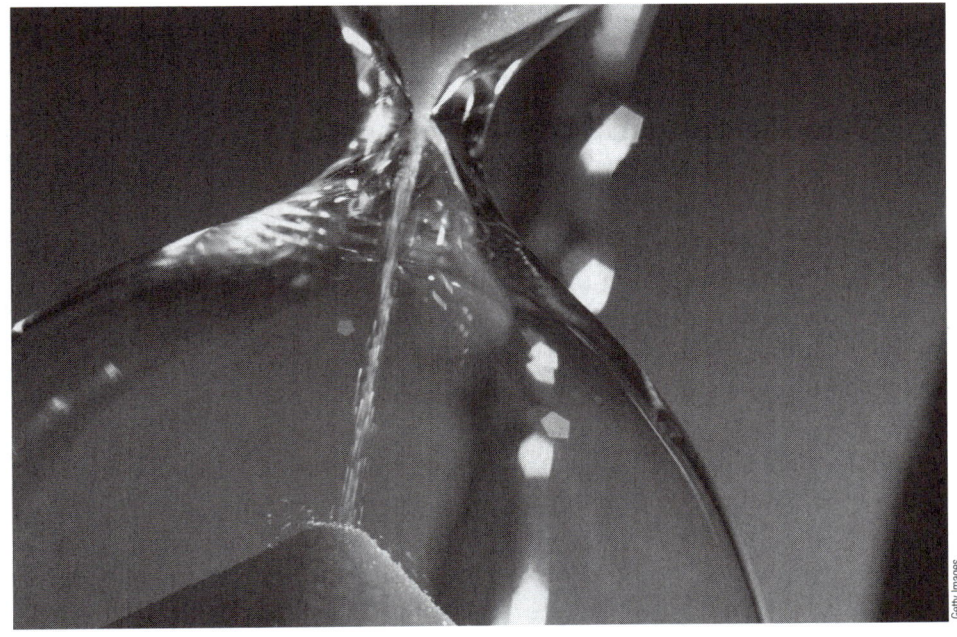

Getty Images

lical understanding about *who* he is and *what* he does. In these verses, John taught three important lessons to help us stand strong against our Savior's archenemy.

1. We learn that antichrists attack Christ (2:18). The Antichrist has a period in which he will reveal himself. The Bible speaks of "last days," "last times," and a "last hour" (2:18). These terms signify the entire period of time between Christ's first and second comings and ring the bell of urgency. We are in that time when antichrists are active because Christ has acted. Without Christ there would be no antichrists. Even *their* coming gives witness to *His* coming.

The Antichrist is a person. John distinguished between antichrists who have come and the antichrist who will come. This one who will come is also the prince mentioned in Daniel 9:27, Paul's man of lawlessness (2 Thess. 2:3), and John's beast out of the sea (Rev. 13:1-10). Satan's superman is on the way.

In 1 and 2 John, the emphasis is on those people who oppose Christ, especially in their teaching. These antichrists think wrongly and believe incorrectly concerning *who Jesus is* and *what Jesus has done.* They get it wrong concerning both His person and His work.

2. We learn that antichrists abandon the church (2:19,22,23). Satan is a master deceiver and strategist. He knows that the best place to launch an attack is from the inside. Once the damage is done, however, antichrists leave the field of battle, taking what captives they can. In doing so, they reveal who they really are.

Physically, they desert the fellowship (2:19). This is no excommunication, but a voluntary exit. John drew both spiritual and theological conclusions: (1) They are lost, and (2) true believers persevere.

Spiritually, they deny the faith (2:22-23, 26). Their physical desertion was divisive but essential. Their spiritual denial is disastrous and heretical, tragic and terrible.

A "liar" is anyone who opposes the truth. What truth? In this context, it is the true Christian doctrine.

They deny the faith by rejecting the Savior. These antichrists denied the reality of both the incarnation (Christ becoming man), and the atonement (Christ's death as a substitute). They claimed Jesus was *important* but not *preeminent, significant* but not the *Savior.*

How are the antichrists active today? Here is one example: Timed to coincide with the 1998 Easter season, the Jesus Seminar published *The Acts Of Jesus: The Search For The Authentic Deeds Of Jesus,* which denies that Jesus was the Son of God, that He was born of a virgin, that He ever performed miracles, that His death was vicarious, atoning for sin, or that He was resurrected.

How do these scholarly skeptics' summations stack up against the convictions of the church throughout its history? Listen to just one voice, the voice of the Council of Nicea in A.D. 325 for a much different judgment:

> "We believe in one God, the Father all-sovereign, maker of heaven and earth, and of all things visible and invisible; and in one Lord Jesus Christ, the Son of God, begotten of the Father, only-begotten, that is, of the substance of the Father, God of God, Light of Light, true God of true God, begotten not made, of one substance with the Father, through whom all things were made, things in heaven and things on the earth; who for us men and for our salvation came down and was made flesh, and became man, suffered, and rose on the third day, ascended into the heavens, is coming to judge living and dead."

Here is a confession John would recognize; here is a Christology he would affirm.

Not only do antichrists reject Jesus, they also reject the Father. John made an amazing affirmation in verses 22-23: "No Son, no Father!" If you do not come to the Son as Savior, you cannot come to God as Father (see 1 Tim. 2:5). As narrow and exclusive as it sounds, Scripture is clear: You cannot have God without believing in Jesus.

This has incredible ramifications for evangelism. It settles the spiritual status of both non-Christian religions and cults. Apart from Jesus as personal Savior and Lord, they are lost. All need to receive, as Savior, the Son of God, Jesus of Nazareth (John 14:6, Acts 4:12).

3. We learn that antichrists assault the Christian (2:20-21,24-25, 27-28). Antichrist and his army are committed to our defeat. Yet, God, in His grace, gives us in these next few verses a three-prong defense that is certain to give us victory.

a. We experience the anointing of the Spirit (2:20-21,27). The word "anointing" is used in connection with the reception of the Spirit (see John 14:17; 15:26; 16:13; 2 Cor. 1:21ff) and implies consecrating and a setting aside of something for a sacred purpose. The Spirit, through the anointing, "teaches you about all things." Our anointing enables us to decipher truth from lies.

Verse 27 can be confusing. The Bible constantly advocates teaching (Matt. 28:20; 1 Cor. 12:28; Eph. 4:11; Col. 3:16; 1 Tim. 4:11; 2 Tim. 2:2, 24), but Gnostic teachers were insisting that the teaching of the apostles was to be supplemented with "higher knowledge" that they (the Gnostics) claimed to possess. John's response was that what the readers were taught under the Spirit's ministry through the apostles not only was adequate but was the only reliable truth. The teaching ministry of the Holy Spirit (what we call illumination) does not involve revelation of *new* truth. Rather, it is the enablement to appropriate God's truth already revealed. All things necessary for salvation are ours; we need nothing more.

b. We embrace the authority of the Scriptures (2:24). The Spirit and the Scriptures are an unbeatable team. In His work of illumination, the Spirit takes the inspired Scriptures and applies them to our lives. We need no additional word. This is where we should "remain."

c. We enjoy remaining in the Son (2:24-25,28). The term "remain" (or "abide") is a favorite of John's. It's used by him more than all the other New Testament writers combined (23 in 1 John; 7 in 2:18-28). The term includes union and communion. When we come to Jesus, we've come home. We're where we need to be. John noted three marvelous blessings which we receive:

The Father: God is Father, Abba. He loves us and cares about us.

Eternal Life: Both the quality and quantity of our

lives are changed. It is life now and forever. It is the very life of God.

Confidence at His Coming: When He comes, we will be ready.

The case is clear: You are either pro-Christ or anti-Christ; you are for Him or against Him. The choice is yours, the decision of eternal significance. Don't be led astray or deceived. Jesus is the Savior. Come to the Son and come today. You'll not be disappointed.

For Your Consideration

1. In what ways do antichrists attempt to disrupt God's coming Kingdom?

2. Why is it important to have a proper understanding of Jesus Christ? Why must Jesus be accepted as Lord and not simply a "good teacher"? Do you treat Jesus as Lord, or merely as a "good teacher"?

3. We are told in 2:18 that we're living in the "last hour." We will be confronted with much false doctrine during this time. What are some things you can do to be better equipped to defend yourself and others against false teaching?

Learning Activity

True Commitment

Complete the following activity. Answer truthfully by placing a "T" for true or "F" for false in the blanks below.

____1. The world's value system entices me to sin.

____2. The world's value system holds little power over my life.

____3. I consider myself committed to Christ and His teachings.

____4. I live my life with the urgency of knowing we are in the last days.

____5. I do not allow others to pull me "off task" from following Christ.

____6. My actions and my attitudes never disrupt the Christian fellowship of our congregation.

____7. I live my life as "set apart" for service to my Lord and Savior Jesus Christ.

____8. I rely on the Holy Spirit to help me on a daily basis.

CHAPTER FOUR

Remain in Him

BIBLE TRUTH: *Remaining in a close relationship with God leads His children to live purely and to avoid sin.*

LIFE IMPACT: *To help you continue in a close relationship with God*

Children of God
(1 John 2:28-3:3)

Family *resemblance* is a powerful evidence of family *relationship*. Children often look like their parents, think like their parents, talk like their parents, and act like their parents.

Children of God are no different. Those who know God as Father look, think, talk, and act like the Savior. As 1 John 2:29 teaches, we've been born of Him, born again, born from above. Those who have been born of God will abide in God—they'll behave like God.

John has challenged us to: walk in the light (1:5-2:2), obey the commandments (2:3-11), know our spiritual status (2:12-14), and beware of the enemies of the faith (2:15-28). Now he says: "Live like children of God." He put four challenges before us.

1. We are to be confident at His coming (2:28-29). First John 2:28 con-

DesignPics

nects verses 18-27 and 2:29–3:3. These passages are tied together by the theme "remaining." However, a new theme is introduced in verse 28 which will run throughout the remainder of the book—the theme of being "born of God." John will use the word 10 times in 2:29–5:21, which is remarkable considering that it doesn't appear once in 1:1–2:28. John says we abide in Christ because we have been born of God; and because we have been born of God, we can be confident at His coming.

The Greek word for "coming" is *parousia* and was sometimes used to describe the arrival of a king, ruler, or official with open public splendor, dignity, and respect. John anticipated the glorious appearing of our King Jesus. Hebrews 9:28 says, "So also the Messiah, having been offered once to bear the sins of many, will appear a second time, not to bear sin, but to bring salvation to those who are waiting for Him." When He comes, how will you react: confident or cowardly? thrilled or timid? rejoicing or regretful?

a. We are to be confident because of our position (2:28). When Christ appears, some people will not be confident; they'll be put to shame in the coming judgment (see Mark 8:38). However, our position with Christ—as fellow heirs to the Kingdom of God—gives us confidence, and we demonstrate that confidence by "remaining in Him." Remaining in Him, we obtain union and communion with both Christ and one another along with our salvation and sanctification. In contrast to a slave going to his master, we approach God as a child coming to his father.

b. *We can also be confident in our practice (2:29)*. Those who continually practice righteousness give evidence of their spiritual birth in Him. We are taught how to *experience* the new birth in John 1:12-13, and we're taught the *evidences* of the new birth in 1 John 2:29. The evidence given here is that of righteous living. Faith always precedes behavior, but right behavior will always follow faith. Why? Because children of God resemble the character of their Father. The righteous Father produces righteous children.

2. *We are to be certain we are His children (3:1)*. John was overwhelmed at the love of God for sinners. That God would bring us into His family and be our Father was something to shout about! The term "how great" conjures up a sense of wonder, awe, amazement, and astonishment. It originally meant "of what country." You see, God's love is not of this world! John noted three evidences of this amazing love:

a. We *have a new Father*: The term "Father" is placed last in Greek text for emphasis—this is a *Father's* love!

b. We *have a new family*: We bear both a new name and a new nature. Once a slave to sin, we're now children of God.

c. We *have a new foe*: The world does not know us (recognize, understand) because it doesn't know Christ. The world hates us because it hates Christ (John 15:18-19).

3. *We are to be conformed to His character (3:2)*. John was again tender in his address ("Dear Friends" or "Beloved") but powerful in his challenge. God saved us not just to take us to heaven but to make us like Jesus. John said it is a signed, sealed, and settled issue in heaven. Again, three reasons are given as to why this is so:

a. We *have an indestructible position*: At this very moment we are children of God, and John included himself in this family. What confidence! I am His, and He is mine.

b. *There is an inevitable revelation*: As the hymn goes, "Blessed assurance Jesus is mine, oh what a foretaste of glory divine." We're not sure of the details of His coming, but we are sure that He will in fact come!

Learning Activity

The Glory of Sonship

Compare the following passages. List in the space below how they are similar in their approach to being a child of God.

1 John 3:1-3	Romans 8:12-17	John 1:12

It's not a matter of "if," but "when."

c. There will be an incredible transformation: We shall be like Him and see Him as He is.

4. We are to be committed to consecration (3:3). The wonderful promise that we will see Him and be like Him should have a present, immediate effect on each of us. We possess a glorious hope—a hope set on Jesus and no other. Whatever Jesus can provide, that is what you will receive.

Such a promise should motivate us to pursue holiness. Our devotion to Jesus should involve purifying

our lives. "Purity" implies being free from contamination, to withdraw from the profane (John 11:55; Jas. 4:8; 1 Pet. 1:22). Hope for the future will produce holiness in the present.

How is this hope to be sought? Colossians 3:1-4 instructs us to "seek what is above." We are to set our minds on divine things, not on things on the earth. Be heavenly minded. It is the only way to be of any earthly good.

To become like Jesus is worth pursuing more than anything else; for every other passion and ambition pales in comparison. Nicholas Von Zinzendorf, founder of the Moravians said it well, "I have one passion only: It is He [Jesus]!"

For Your Consideration
1. Why can believers approach God boldly (2:28)?

2. Why does it seem that our world does not understand the life and thoughts of Christians?

3. How does the fact that Christians are now "children of God" change the way they live? What is the mandate for this change?

Truth About Sin
(1 John 3:4-10)

John Chrysostom (A.D. 344–407) was the bishop of Constantinople and one of the greatest preachers to ever live. So powerful was his preaching that he earned the name *Chrysostomos* meaning "golden mouthed." Tradition has it that he was arrested by the Roman emperor, who unsuccessfully sought to make John recant his alleged heresies.

After discussing with his advisers what could be done to the prisoner, the emperor asked, "Shall I put him in a dungeon?" "No," one replied, "for he will be glad to go. He longs for the quietness wherein he can delight in the mercies of his God." "Then I'll execute him!" said the emperor. "No," was the answer, "for he will also be glad to die. He declares that in the event of death he will be in the presence of the Lord." "What shall we do then?" the ruler asked. "There's only one thing that will cause Chrysostom to suffer," the counselor said. "Make him

A CLOSER LOOK

The Devil

Devil *(diabolos)* means accuser or slanderer. Satan, from the Hebrew, *Satan,* means adversary. When he first sinned we don't know. We only know that it occurred before Genesis 3, possibly even before the creation of Adam and Eve. He's been sinning "from the beginning." Satan is the source of sin. He is its originator, its instigator. Those who live in and enjoy the world of sin give irrefutable evidence that they are his children. The devil's fall is hinted at in Isaiah 14:12-15, which also records the fall of the king of Babylon, and in Ezekiel 28:11-15, which records the fall of the king of Tyre.

sin. He's afraid of nothing except sin." What a testimony and witness!

The apostle John knew that our attitude toward sin is important. It gives evidence of whether we are a child of God or of Satan. John saw no middle ground on this. If you love sin and sin is your life, you're a child of Satan. If you love righteousness and righteousness is your life, you're a child of God. John made this clear in 2:29 and 3:3. Then he drove home that truth again as he divided the world of humanity into two categories, two families: "children of God" and "children of Satan."

Looking at things from the child of God's perspective, John addressed three subjects: (1) the wickedness of sin; (2) the work of the Savior; and (3) the walk of the saint.

1. Recognize the wickedness of sin (3:4,7,8). John began with the problem that plagues all of humanity—sin. He defined and described sin.

a. Sin is disobedience (3:4). In 2:29, John spoke of those who practice what is right. In 3:4 John spoke of those who break the law. The term he used refers to a willful rejection and an active disobedience against God's moral standard. It's a clenched fist saying no to God in attitude and action and is a characteristic of a child of the devil.

b. Sin is deceptive (3:7). The word "deceive" means to lead astray and recalls the previous warning of 2:26. The false teachers attempt to lead us astray both doctrinally (concerning the Savior) and morally (concerning sin). They minimize sin, if not deny it all together.

John counterpunched: The one who practices (lives a life of) righteousness is in fact righteous. He will act out who he is. The practice of righteousness is the evidence that we are righteous.

Do not be deceived. If you belong to Christ, you will follow and imitate Him (2:6). Here's the difference: The lost person will occasionally do what is right but will continually sin. The saved person will continually do what is right but occasionally sin. Jesus reminded us in Matthew 7:16, "You will know them by their fruit."

c. Sin is of the devil (3:8). For the first time in the letter, John referred directly to the devil (3:12; 2:13-14, 5:18-19). John exposed Satan's threefold strategy to defeat humanity. Satan operates as a liar (intellectual sabotage; John 8:44), as a sinner (moral sabotage; 1 John 3:8), and as a killer (physical sabotage; John 8:44).

Here in 3:8, John made plain that those who live a life of sin provide evidence that the devil is their spiritual father. His nature is their nature; his actions are their actions.

2. Remember the work of the Savior (3:5,8). John exposed the truth about both sin and Satan, along with those who live for and love sin. Then, he moved to examine the truth about the Savior. Since sin and Satan are our problem, Jesus provides an answer, a solution, for both. How?

a. Jesus delivers us from sin (3:5). John again made clear a basic theological truth: Jesus could do what He did because He was who He was. What did He do? He "was revealed"—implying His preexistence—to take away our sin.

John taught that Jesus is the righteous One (2:29), the pure One (3:3), and the sinless One (3:5). Second Corinthians 5:21 reads, "He made the One who did not know sin to be sin for us, so that we might become the righteousness of God in Him." Hebrews 4:15 teaches, "For we do not have a High Priest who is unable to sympathize with our weaknesses, but One who has been tested in every way as we are, yet without sin."

b. Jesus also destroys the work of Satan (3:8b). The phrase "Son of God," which occurs 7 times in the letter (3:8; 4:15; 5:5,10,12,13,20), emphasizes the divine nature of Jesus Christ. Only He could have stepped onto the stage of human history and dealt with our archenemy.

This was the purpose of Jesus' first coming—to "destroy the Devil's works." Victory over Satan is one aspect of the multifaceted work of Christ. He's our satisfaction, justification, redemption, and reconciliation. He's our Victor, the One who has set us free from captivity. By invading the enemies' territory, He dealt Satan a deathblow at Calvary, the empty tomb an eternal monument of His victory (Heb. 2:14).

3. Rejoice in the walk of the saint (3:6,9,10). John instructed us on sin, Satan, and the Savior. Then, John painted a picture of the life that has been set free from sin and delivered from Satan. John pointed out three wonderful blessings Christians possess:

a. We enjoy a new liberty (3:6). Verse 6 logically flows from 3:5: Because there is no sin in Jesus, there will be no sin in the child of God. Now, what exactly does that mean? Was John contradicting what he said in 1:8 and 1:10? Numerous interpretations of this verse have been posited. They include:

Christians are sinless and perfect in their new nature.

Christians do not commit certain sins (for example, the sins of the false teachers).

John was describing the ideal.

Christians do not commit willful or deliberate sin.

Christians, when abiding in Christ, do not sin.

The Christian does not commit habitual sin.

This last view emphasizes in this context a continual action ("does not keep on sinning") and is the most satisfactory explanation. Set free from the bondage of sin and Satan, God's children won't live in continual sin and rebellion. He may periodically fall into sin, but he will not walk in it. It no longer dominates his life. It's the exception, not the rule.

In contrast, those who do live in sin reveal that they have neither *seen* nor *known* Christ. They have never spiritually envisioned the Savior so as to know Him in a personal, saving relationship. Sin and Satan are their life, not righteousness and Jesus.

b. We also enjoy a new life (3:9). "Born of God" speaks of a past action with continuing results. It looks to the new birth of our regeneration (conversion). The believer cannot continue in sin because of the divine nature he receives through the new birth. Jesus said in John 3:3, "I assure you: Unless someone is born again, he cannot see the kingdom of God" (see also 2 Cor. 5:17). Believers are freed from the bondage of sin.

c. We enjoy a new love (3:10). This verse summarizes a discussion that began in 2:3. It also prepares us for a more extended discussion to follow. Two tests are set forth that distinguish a child of God from a child of the devil: Do you practice righteousness? Do you love others?

Those who hate sin—those born of God and set free from the devil—will practice righteousness and love others. This is what God does, and this is what His children will do. You see, children have the distinguishing marks of their parents. Children look and act like their parents. What they see their Father do, they do also. What we see our Savior do, we will naturally do as well.

For Your Consideration

1. For what purpose was Christ "revealed"?

2. What factors distinguish children of God from children of Satan?

3. On a scale of 1-10, how would you rate your lifestyle in the following areas:

   remaining in Christ (2:28; 3:9) ____

   anticipating His coming (2:28) ____

   purifying self (3:3) ____

   practicing righteousness (3:7) ____

   Dedicate yourself over the next week to strengthening those areas of your life.

Love One Another

BIBLE TRUTH: *Believers demonstrate their love for God by putting love for others into action.*

LIFE IMPACT: *To help you serve others sacrificially*

Love and Hate
(1 John 3:11-15)

In 1965, Jackie de Shannon debuted a song that would rise to number 4 on the pop charts. The words of the first two lines are familiar even today: "What the world needs now is love, sweet love. It's the only thing that there's just too little of. What the world needs now is love, sweet love. No not just for some, but for everyone." Although we might debate the phrase, "it's the *only thing* that there's just too little of," we could all agree that the world could use a little more love. However, this isn't anything new. The world has needed more love since the beginning of time, as our text makes painfully clear.

First John 3:11 begins a new discussion and theme. Compare 1:5 with 3:11. They both begin with "This is the message." In 1:5 the message is

Learning Activity
Moral Opposites

Work in small groups and scan each of the Scripture passages listed below. In the space provided, describe the importance placed on one's attitude in each Scripture text.

1 John 3:12 and 3:15

Matthew 5:21-22

Matthew 5:27-28

Mark 7:18-23

"God is light;" in 3:11 the message is "Love one another." So the focus shifts from "God is light" to "God is love."

Now, it's fair to ask: Why should we love one another? John gives an answer: we have a *message which commands love,* and there is *a murderer who contradicts love.*

1. We have a message that commands love (3:11). Verse 10 states that if you do not love your brother (neighbor), you are not a child of God, but a child of the devil. For this reason (and what follows), we must heed the command to love.

a. Love is essential. John said that the absence of love in the lives of his converted readers is inconsistent with the message proclaimed to them from the beginning. Love is grounded in the very nature of God (4:7-8) and was taught by Christ Himself (John 13:34-35; 15:12,17). John called for a continuous display of love in the family of God. It's a challenge which never dies; it never grows old. It's not optional; it's essential.

b. Love is personal. This is our all-encompassing assignment: Love continually, and love individually; no favorites, no bias, and no discrimination here. It is not love some, many, most, or almost all. No, love them all—even those who hurt you, ignore you, and mistreat you. Our lives should also be characterized by a personal love for others (3:11).

2. There is a murderer who contradicts love (3:12-15). John looked back to history's first example of an unloving act: the murder of Abel by his brother Cain. We see that we often murder in two ways: by action and by attitude. Both are unbecoming of God's children.

a. We shouldn't murder by action (3:12-13). Verse 12 stands in stark contrast to the end of verse 11. Cain's actions revealed his true spiritual father, the devil (John 8:44). To *murder* means to butcher or slay (literally, to cut the throat). It's a violent, brutal killing with motives rooted in an evil heart. Abel's righteous acts first provoked *jealousy* in Cain, then *hatred*, then *murder*—a natural and terrible sequence. Cain's hatred of Abel illustrates the age-old conflict between good and evil, between God-inspired love and Satan-inspired hatred. Satan always has hated God's children; and since the world belongs to him, it should come as no surprise when the children of the world hate you. Remember Jesus' words in John 15:18, "If the world hates you, understand that it hated Me before it hated you." It's natural for the world to hate us because their father hates us. John instructed us to be different. Don't be like them. Turn the other cheek. Love the unlovable.

b. Neither should we murder in attitude (3:14-15).
The love we show others is a test case of our spiritual
condition. Loving others continually out of gratitude
for all that Jesus has done for us (v. 16) gives proof that
we have passed from spiritual death into spiritual life
(John 5:24).

Eternal life is not *earned* by loving others; rather, it's
the *evidence* that eternal life is ours. The negative
corollary is also clear: if you do not love others, the
absence of love proves that you remain spiritually
dead. In fact, a hateful attitude is equivalent to murder!
This is mentioned four times in 3:12 and 3:15. John's
reasoning followed the pattern of our Lord's teaching
on adultery in Matthew 5:27-28, and it's reminiscent of
Matthew 5:21-22 where Jesus said, "You have heard
that it was said to our ancestors, 'Do not murder, and
whoever murders will be subject to judgment.' But I
tell you, everyone who is angry with his brother will be
subject to judgment." Love and hate are moral oppo-
sites. John said that without love, we have no life.

For Your Consideration
1. Why is Christian love essential?

2. What's the difference between murdering in action
   and murdering in attitude? Is one worse than the
   other? Why or why not?

Learning Activity

Loving God, Loving Others

Read 1 John 3:16-24 and complete the statements below.

• God has shown His love to me by …

• I have shown God's love to others by …

• I can show compassion to those that have less than me by …

Love in Action
(1 John 3:16-24)

If the demonstration of love is the evidence that one is a child of God, then what does this love look like? John set before us, in 3:16-24, the supreme example: the sacrifice of the Son of God. This is easily seen by comparing John 3:16 with 1 John 3:16. John 3:16 says that God gave His Son *for us*. First John 3:16 says that we should give ourselves *for others*. You want to see true love? Look no farther than the cross!

Jesus' sacrifice proves His love for us (3:16). Jesus' love was proven by His conscious and willful act on Calvary. He could give no greater gift and make no greater sacrifice. Sin nailed Jesus to the cross, but love kept Jesus on the cross.

Similarly, our sacrifice proves our love for Him: "We should also" (3:16) entails moral obligation. Just like He died for us, we should be willing to die for others. Just like He put it all on the line for us, we should be willing to put it all on the line for others (John 15:13). We have an obligation (a mandate) to follow the example of our Lord.

How is the sacrificial life seen among believers?

1. We are to be generous with our possessions (3:17). If Christ's love resides in someone and that person sees another believer in need, will he not help him? Generosity originates in the heart, and the heart controls the hand! John was concerned with a lack of love. Dead hearts and dead words go together, but a redeemed heart and sacrificial love likewise go hand in hand.

2. We are told to put our money where our mouth is (3:18). John made this appeal based on their common spiritual life and his fatherly care and concern for them. He used a negative-positive line of reasoning: love is more than making a good speech or using impressive

rhetoric (see 1 Cor. 13). Love expresses itself in deeds. Love is an action word! However, truth must be applied to our actions as well because, though words may be empty, actions can be hypocritical. They can be done out of the wrong motives or for the wrong reasons. The love John was talking about is embodied in Jesus' parable recorded in Luke 10:30-37. Take a moment and read this passage.

The great church Father, St. Augustine, once said, "Love Christ with all your heart and do as you please." If we truly love Christ, we will not love others in word only (which is no love at all). We will also love them in deed and in truth, just like Jesus loves us.

After explaining the importance of displaying Christ's love to others, John developed his train of thought by giving characteristics of a true follower of Christ: love, obedience, and faithfulness. Each is vitally important, and each provides the Christian with indispensable gifts from God.

Verse 18 links 3:11-17 with 3:19-24. Love and obedience (as exhibited in 3:11-17) confirms that you are in the truth (3:18), reassures your heart (3:19-20), gives you confidence when you pray (3:21-22), and demonstrates that you abide in Him (3:23-24). Love and truth correspond. Love and confidence correspond. Love and obedience correspond.

1. Love provides acceptance in His presence (3:18-20). When we love others as God in Christ has loved us, *we have certainty in the faith* (3:18-19). By our love we give evidence of our rebirth. Our rebirth, by its very nature, entails the empowering of the Holy Spirit, and the Holy Spirit gives certainty in our faith.

Also, by loving others, we have confidence before the Father (3:19-20). Why? (a) God is greater than our hearts, and (b) He knows all things. When we fail to love in action and truth (3:18), God, who is greater than our hearts and knows all things, deals with us. Our heart rightly judges and condemns us for not genuinely loving others.

Our consciences and our hearts may be either too severe or too lenient in its verdict (1 Cor. 4:3-5). God, however, sees everything, and knows our inward thoughts. Indeed, He knows our hearts better than we know them ourselves. His grace and mercy will help us to love. He will motivate us (3:17) to soften a hard, unloving heart. He will inspire us, encourage us, and challenge us to love others just like He has loved us (3:16). He's the perfect judge. No failure or success escapes His notice. Loving others as He loves us will provide acceptance in His presence.

2. Obedience provides confidence in our prayers (3:21-22). Confidence

A CLOSER LOOK
Conditions for Prayer

John Stott, in his commentary *Letters of John*, lists six conditions that must be met for prayer to be answered. A prayer must be:
- offered in Jesus' name (John 16:23-24)
- for God's glory (Jas. 4:2-3);
- from a heart that doesn't cherish sin (Ps. 66:18);
- from a forgiven and forgiving heart (Mark 11:25);
- with faith (Matt 21:22); and
- backed by an obedient life (1 John 3:22).

toward God (3:21) naturally leads to confidence in prayer (3:22). This confidence is grounded in our love life and based on obedience. We are confident in two ways: in our position and in our petitions.

a. We can be confident in our position (3:21). Verse 21 stands in stark contrast with verse 20. When we commit judgment to God and His Word regarding our heart, thoughts, motives, and actions, He heals our heart, forgives our sins (1:9), reminds us He is our advocate and atonement (2:1-2), and motivates us to love others (3:16). In such a position, we can indeed have confidence and boldness toward God.

b. We can be confident in our petitions (3:22). The key to answered prayer is obedience. When we're disobedient to God, why should we think He will answer us when we pray? (see 1 John 5:14-15; Prov. 15:29.) While the phrase "receive whatever we ask" is all-inclusive, it's also conditional. The one asking must be (a) keeping His commandments and (b) doing what pleases Him. This will regulate and guide our prayer life.

3. Faithfulness provides assurance in our position (3:23-24). These verses are subtly Trinitarian, with the

Father alluded to in 3:23-24, the Son in 3:23, and the Spirit in 3:24. The essence of the gospel is found in these verses as well, which can be summarized as confessing the Son, caring for the saints, and communing with the Spirit. Let's look briefly at each:

a. Confess the Son (3:23). John established here the central command which sums up all the mandates in Scripture. It is, in essence, a two-fold test: (1) "that we believe in the name of His Son Jesus Christ" (the doctrinal test), and (2) that we "love one another" (the moral test). To "believe in Christ" means to place your trust and faith in Him and Him alone. You trust all of Him—not some, part or even most. You trust either the biblical Christ or no Christ at all.

b. Care for the Saints (3:23). As we've seen, faith and love are twin companions. What we believe will impact how we love. John, looking back to the words of Jesus on the night He was betrayed, reminded us that it was Jesus who first gave us the command to love one another (John 13:34-35). If you really and truly believe in Jesus, you will really, truly, genuinely, and actively love one another.

c. *Commune with the Spirit (3:24).* Having the Spirit and remaining in Him also go together. The Bible's view of the Spirit is clear: He is the third person of the one true God. We worship and abide in the Spirit of the living God. He is the Spirit of truth (John 14:16), the Comforter, Counselor (John 14:26), and the One who will guide us into all truth (John 16:13). He comes as a gift and He alone enables us to remain in Christ (Rom. 8:16).

Several years ago, a popular teen magazine ran an article entitled, "Do You Believe in God?" The article drew an avalanche of responses. Several stand out. Below are two responses which contrast a heart of despair with a heart of hope. Note the radically different world views seen in each:

> *I was taught that God was the Almighty and was good, but the past few months have set me straight. There is no God. If He/She was real, then there wouldn't be so much disease, death, hurt and heartbreak in the world. In December, one of my friends lost her mother. In January, a friend was killed on his way to school. In April, a friend of the family lost his long battle with AIDS. And in May, one of my best friends also lost her mother. What God would want to do this to anyone? None that I know of or believe in.*

I was 17 when I left high school, depressed and without direction. I found myself pregnant and married a man who essentially reaffirmed that I was not going to amount to much. I later divorced him and continued making monumentally lousy decisions. Then I met someone, now my best friend. He too is a parent. He began to tell me that I was worth something. He listened as I expressed my disgust with what I had done with my life. At times, I even personally attacked him. But his patience was unbelievable. Today, I am a student in a very competitive medical program and a much better parent. I owe all my success to my best friend, who has been there every step of the way. So what does this have to do with whether I believe in God? Who do you think my best friend is?

There is help for a hurting heart. It's found in a perfect Father, in His Son, and by means of a perfect Spirit in Whom we abide. He'll never let you down or fail you.

True joy is found only when you align yourself with God's plan for humankind. Everything we do should be done with the objective of bringing God glory (1 Cor. 10:31). We glorify Him by obeying Him and loving others. Our focus is always upward because that's where peace is found. That's where help for hurting hearts is found.

For Your Consideration

1. Compare 1 John 3:23-24 with John 13:34-35. How does one "live out" these verses at home, church, and work? Find for yourself *specific* ways in which you can demonstrate your love for Christ by loving others. (Remember, love is action.)

2. In light of 3:20, should your conscience be your guide? Why or why
   not? If not, then what?

3. Read Psalm 139:1-6,23-24. Use verses 23-24 as a prayer to God as He
   searches your heart for "any offensive ways."

Do Not Be Deceived

BIBLE TRUTH: *Believers are to beware of deceptive teachers who reject the truth about Christ and His loving sacrifice for others.*

LIFE IMPACT: *To help you show God's love by telling others of Jesus' sacrifice for our sins*

Truth and Error
(1 John 4:1-6)

"What do you believe about Jesus?" This is life's most crucial question. Yet, no question has received more confusing and mistaken answers. That's certainly true in our day.

John sounded a warning to "test the spirits to determine if they are from God, because many false prophets have gone out into the world" (4:1). He knew that misunderstanding Jesus would lead to misunderstanding other doctrines. John repeatedly taught us by contrast:

Truth verses falsehood (2:18-28)

Children of God verses children of the devil (2:29-3:12)

Love verses hatred (3:11-24)

Then, he added a fourth: the Spirit of God versus the spirit of antichrist (4:1-6). John challenged us to be "spiritual investigators" to determine what's from God and what's not. He provided four tests.

1. We will know false teachers by examination (4:1). John genuinely loved the people to whom he was writing and called them "beloved." By using this term, John's warning was heightened.

a. False teachers serve a different master. Behind every prophet and proclamation is a spirit. However, not all spirits are from God, and "testing the spirits" is the only way to discover their genuineness. Watch how they act: do they act like Christ? Listen to what they say: do they proclaim Jesus as the only Savior, the perfect Son of God? If not, reject them.

b. False teachers are deceptive in their message. There is a tendency to ascribe any unusual phenomenon to God. Such a lack of discernment opens the door for false teaching and provides an opportunity for demonic activity to invade the church. Remember, religious activity is not necessarily godly activity. Watch and wait. Look and listen. Evaluate the message by Scripture. False prophets are deceptive in their message (see Deut. 13:1-5; Deut. 18:20-22; 2 Cor. 11:1-4). Jesus warned us (Matt. 7:15; 24:11, 14; Mark 13:21-23), Paul warned us (Acts 20:28-30), Peter warned us (2 Pet. 2:1-22), and Jude warned us (Jude 4-19).

2. We will know them by their confession (4:2-3). In Matthew 16:13 Jesus asked His disciples: "Who do people say that the Son of Man is?" Humanity can be divided into two categories: those who answer correctly and those who answer wrongly.

a. Faithful teachers declare the truth about Jesus (4:2). The Spirit of God always honors Jesus (John 16:14). Christianity stands or falls on the truth of God's Son becoming flesh in the person of Jesus. This truth isn't optional; it's essential. Amazingly, even demons recognized the deity of Jesus (Mark 1:24; 3:4; 5:7-8). It's a sad commentary that some demons have a better theology than do some pastors, teachers, and theologians.

b. False teachers deny the truth about Jesus (4:3). Verse 3 is the antithesis of verse 2. When it comes to what people believe about Jesus, the 1st century was a lot like the 21st century. Already there were people who refused to believe the truth about God sending His Son.

The Docetists said Jesus was a phantom or spirit who only *appeared* to be human. A man named Cerenthius said God's Spirit empowered the human Jesus at His baptism but left Him before the crucifixion.

The false teachers denied the reality of the incarnation, the wedding of deity and humanity in the person of Jesus. Those who deny the truth of Christ's incarnation are not from God, but from the Antichrist. The spirit of antichrist (a term meaning "against Christ") was active in John's day, he's active in our day, and he will remain active until Jesus comes again.

3. We know them by their identification (4:4-5). John tenderly encouraged his "little children" by declaring the victory God has provided for them. With His help, John said they've overcome the lying prophets and

A CLOSER LOOK

Jesus

On June 14, 2000 Southern Baptists adopted as their Confession the Baptist Faith and Message 2000. Here is what we confess about Jesus:

"Christ is the eternal Son of God. In His incarnation as Jesus Christ, He was conceived of the Holy Spirit and born of the virgin Mary. Jesus perfectly revealed and did the will of God, taking upon Himself human nature with its demands and necessities and identifying Himself completely with mankind yet without sin. He honored the divine law by His personal obedience, and in His substitutionary death on the cross. He made provision for the redemption of men from sin. He was raised from the dead with a glorified body and appeared to His disciples as the person who was with them before His crucifixion. He ascended into heaven and is now exalted at the right hand of God where He is the One Mediator, fully God, fully man, in whose Person is effected the reconciliation between God and man. He will return in power and glory to judge the world and to consummate His redemptive mission. He now dwells in all believers as the living and ever present Lord."

Learning Activity
False Prophets

Read the following Scriptures which give warning of false prophets. Paraphrase the passages in the space provided.

• Matthew 7:15-19

• Mark 13:21-23

• Acts 20:28-30

their spirit of antichrist. Here he contrasted faithful teachers with unfaithful ones:

a. Faithful teachers have a foundation in God (4:4). He's the source of our strength, comfort, confidence, and security. John explained that the reason we've "conquered" these false teachers is that "the One who is in [us] is greater than the one who is in the world." Satan, Antichrist, and the false prophets are no match for the Father and His Christ. Believers should be alert to false teaching, but they shouldn't be afraid.

b. False teachers have a congregation of the world (4:5). In contrast to Christians, false teachers are "from the world," referring to Satan's domain. They speak like the world, and the world hears them. Such teaching is attractive to people of the world. What might such messages sound like? Here are some examples:

"All religions are the same."

"Jesus is a good way but not the only way."

"Jews, Muslims, and Buddhists don't need to be evangelized."

"One way religion is an evil religion."

The world applauds this type of teaching. It may be politically correct and popular, but it's spiritually corrupt and deadly. Remember, the key to identifying true teachers from false ones is to listen for their beliefs about Jesus.

4. We know the spirit of the Antichrist by their corruption (4:6). John's teaching in 4:6 is reflective of Jesus' warning found in John 8:47, "He who is of God hears God's words; therefore you do not hear, because you are not of God." Faithful people reject the teachings of the world (of the Antichrist) and welcome the Word of God and what it teaches about Jesus.

False prophets hate God's word. Lost, unregenerate, and unbelieving people do not believe, welcome, or appreciate true teaching. They embody the "spirit of deception."

For Your Consideration

1. In what three ways are we to recognize false doctrine?

2. John wrote that "the One who is in you is greater than the one who is in the world." What does this mean?

3. What significance does 1 John 4:4 have in your life? Spend a moment reflecting on this verse. Thank God for supplying you with the Holy Spirit to protect you from false doctrine.

God's Love and Ours
(1 John 4:7-21)

A group of children aged 4-8 were asked the following question: "What does love mean?" Their answers were funny and much broader and deeper than originally anticipated. According to kids, "love is…"
- "when you go out to eat and give somebody most of your French fries without making them give you any of theirs."
- "when my mommy makes coffee for my daddy and she takes a sip before giving it to him, to make sure the taste is OK."
- "when you tell a guy you like his shirt, then he wears it everyday."
- "when mommy gives daddy the best piece of chicken."
- "You really shouldn't say 'I love you' unless you mean it; but if you mean it, you should say it a lot. People forget."

Well, it is one thing to get a child's perspective on love, but it is even better to get God's. We find it in 1 Corinthians 13 and here in 1 John 4:7-21. While Paul is often called the apostle of faith, James the apostle

of works, and Peter the apostle of hope, John was perhaps the expert on love. He addressed the subject in
2:7-11 as an indication that one is "walking in the
light" and again in 3:11-24 as evidence that one is a
"child of God."

Yet it's in 4:7-21 that we see his most thorough
explanation. In fact, the word "love" dominates
4:7-5:3, appearing 32 times (43 times in the entire letter). John asks, "How is your love life?" The only way
to answer is to measure our love against the standard of
God's love. Verses 7-21 give us seven characteristics of
God's love.

1. God's love is specific (4:7). Beginning again with
his tender phrase, "Dear friends," John transitioned
from the subject of false prophets (4:1-6) to the subject of love (4:7-21). The passage peaks both in 4:8 and
in 4:16, where John twice declared, "God is love."

John emphasized love as a personal responsibility:
"Let us love one another." "Us" is plural, and "one
another" is both personal and reciprocal. You can't
force others to love, and someone else can't love others *for* you.

A CLOSER LOOK

Only Begotten

We get the phrase "only begotten" (4:9) from the Greek
word *monogenes.* It occurs 9 times in the New Testament
and 5 times in John's letters (John 1:14,18; 3:16, 18; 1
John 4:9). It speaks of His utter uniqueness. There is none
like Him. He's one of a kind. As God's "Son," he is the joy
of the Father's heart. He loves him like no other (John
3:25; 5:20). This fact should highlight how great the
Father's love is for us!

2. *God's love is supernatural (4:7-8)*. John knew that it's just not in our nature to love all people all of the time in our own strength and ability. But remember what 4:4 says: the greater One in us also *enables* us to love another. God helps us to love, and doing so provides evidence of two very wonderful truths.

a. *Love shows you are born of God (4:7)*. Love has its source in God. Those demonstrating divine love give proof of their new birth.

b. *Love shows you know God (4:7-8)*. Having been born again, we *keep on* knowing God. We grow in our knowledge and understanding of Him—especially in the truth that "He is love."

3. *God's love is visible (4:9-10)*. Christians too often fail to love as they ought because they fail to recall what God has done. First John 4:9 is reminiscent of John 3:16 and 1 John 3:16, which say that the love of God was manifested (made clear) to us (helpless sinners) that we may live through Him. Spiritual life is reserved only for those who come to God by Christ and His cross.

That the Father would sacrifice His Son is a repulsive concept to many people today. For example one liberal theologian claimed that Jesus' death was the ultimate form of child abuse—that the cross depicts God as an abusive parent and Jesus as the obedient, trusting child. God's Word sees it differently. Christ's death was absolutely necessary; for through His death, sin was atoned for, and God's love was proven and shown once and for all.

4. *God's love is satisfying (4:11-12)*. Verses 11-12 describe a great motivation for the Christian to love. Looking back to verses 9-10, John said, "If God loved us in this way, we also must love one another." The inclusion of "must" involves an inner compulsion and a moral obligation. The example of God's love in sending and sacrificing His Son teaches and inspires us to love.

We also experience maturity through love (4:12). The word "seen" implies a close scrutiny or examination. No person has seen God "up close and personal" in His unveiled glory. While no one can completely see God, people can see His love demonstrated through Christian believers!

5. *God's love is spiritual (4:13-14)*. Verses 13-14 have a distinct Trinitarian flavor. First, note the reference to the Spirit (4:13). Believers can and should have an ongoing awareness that we are in God and He is in us (Rom. 5:5; 8:16; 1 Cor 6:19). His presence in our lives is proof we belong to God and proof that God's love is spiritual.

DesignPics

We then see a clear reference to the Father and Son (4:14). No one has seen the Father, but we have seen the Son He sent. This is why He came: to demonstrate the power of His love by becoming the Savior of the world.

6. God's love is confident (4:15-18). Because of Jesus, we know God both lives in us and unconditionally loves us. While faith gives us this assurance, faith demands an object. How do we know God's love? By sending His Son and Spirit, He enables us to love others just as He has loved us. Faith and love are simultaneously fruit and evidence of one who is indwelt by God. John was certain of God's love.

We are to "remain in love." Doing so is proof that God remains in us. This reciprocal and mutual relationship is spiritual and tangible, supernatural and yet visible. The Christian can stand confidently before God without any need to fear the day of judgment (fear is mentioned four times in 4:18). The torment associated

Learning Activity
Love Comparison

Work with your neighbor and read the following Scripture passages: 1 John 4:7-21 and 1 Corinthians 13. Answer the following questions.

1. How do the two authors agree?

2. How do they differ?

3. How is love supreme in both?

with being unprepared to meet God as judge vanishes because we have God's perfect love abiding in us. Love brings us rest, peace, and confidence.

7. God's love gives us a command (4:19-21). Verse 19 is crucial: Yes, we love, but He loved first. Our love owes its origin to God's love. God took the initiative. We respond to the love He showed first.

Verse 20 introduces a hypothetical, "If anyone says." John understood that character is proven by action. Love for God and hatred for a brother cannot coexist in the same heart. They are incompatible and cannot live together. Loving your brother whom you can see is proof that you love God whom you cannot see. To do otherwise is to be a liar.

In 4:21, John summarized Jesus' command heard in Mark 12:30-31: Love God and love your brothers and sisters in the faith. This is not merely a suggestion, but a command.

When terrorists killed thousands of Americans on September 11, 2001, *Newsweek* carried a story in which they said of the hijacking terrorists, "All that is known for certain is that the hijackers had holes in their souls that many Americans cannot begin to fathom but that Bin Laden and his minions knew how to fill" (Oct. 22, 2001).

Actually, there is no great mystery here. There's a difference between someone who knows God's love in Christ and someone who doesn't; between someone who has seen God in Christ and someone who hasn't; between someone in whom God's love is being perfected and someone in whom Satanic hatred is being perfected. It's the difference between someone in love with an Osama Bin Laden and someone in love with the Lord Jesus Christ.

The Bible teaches that there is great power in love. If love is real, you'll be able to see it even in the most difficult places of life. Love is the proof the Holy Spirit of God is at work in your life.

For Your Consideration

1. What is the relationship between the phrases "that we might live through Him" (4:9) and "the propitiation for our sins" (4:10)?

2. Is the Christian mandated to love others? Why or why not?

3. Why is loving others often so difficult?

CHAPTER SEVEN

Keep on Trusting Jesus

BIBLE TRUTH: *Those whose faith is in Jesus overcome the evils of this life and confidently face the coming judgment.*

LIFE IMPACT: *To help you live confidently by continuing to trust in Jesus*

Faith's Victory
(1 John 5:1-13)

For years American sports fans tuned into ABC's "Wide World of Sports." The show spanned the globe, bringing into our homes sports of every imaginable variety. Yet who can forget the tragic fall of Vinko Bogataj, the Yugoslavian ski jumper whose horrific crash found him forever attached to the phrase, "The thrill of victory and the agony of defeat!" That's the way it is in sports. There will always be winners and losers—those who seize victory and those who taste defeat.

The apostle John was determined that his spiritual children taste the thrill of victory and avoid the agony of defeat. Just as athletes need strength, speed, skill, and training, John knew Christians need a new birth, love, obedience, and faith. Indeed John was committed to the proposition that "faith in Christ equals victory."

God wants us to experience this victory that overcomes the world; and in our text, John presented six ways in which Christians experience victory.

1. Christians experience victory by believing in Jesus (5:1). Although the theme of love is continued from 4:7-21, the emphasis in the following verses shifts to belief and faith. This focus on faith is two-fold. We must first know in whom to believe. Spiritual victory comes from placing faith in—and only in—Jesus. We're not to put our hope in Peter, James, or John. Our faith is not in Joseph Smith, Mohammed, or Buddha. The sole object of our believing is Jesus.

Learning Activity
His Yoke is Easy

Work with your neighbor and compare John's writing in 1 John 5:3-5 with Jesus' teachings in Matthew 11:28-30 and Luke 11:46. Complete the statements in the space below.

• John's writing agrees with Jesus' teaching in that . . .

• Jesus' teachings were different from the scribes and Pharisees because . . .

• In my stressful world, John's writings and Jesus' teachings are a comfort because . . .

We also should know what to believe. First John instructs us to believe that Jesus is:
- the Word of Life (1:1)
- our advocate and atonement (2:1-2)
- God in the flesh (4:2)
- the propitiation for our sins (4:10)
- God's Son (4:14)
- the Savior of the World (4:14).

Belief in Jesus is mental, emotional, volitional, and even ethical. It involves the whole person. It's no mere intellectual assent, but rather it is trusting all that you are to all that He is. Our belief should echo Peter's confession in Matthew 16:16, "You are the Christ, the Son of the living God" (see 1 John 5:1, 5).

2. Christians experience victory by loving others (5:1-2). In the Bible (and especially in 1 John) faith and love are inseparable (see 3:23). Both are vitally connected to spiritual birth (see John 3). Those born of God are called to love the Father, the Son, and their brothers and sisters in the family of God.

If you love God the Father, you will also love His children. The last part of 5:1 ("loves his child.") should not be restricted to Jesus; it should not exclude Him either. In loving our heavenly Father, we will naturally love His Son, Jesus. In fact, to love one and not the other is a thought unimaginable to John.

The Christian will not only love Jesus; he will love all of God's children. Love for others is grounded in our love of God, for our love for God is demonstrated in our obedience to Him, and one of His commandments is to love others (3:11, 4:7,12,21). However, before you can love your brother or sister on earth, you must first love your Father in heaven.

3. Christians experience victory by obeying God (5:2-3). The concepts of love and obedience are never to be separated. In believing God, we obey God. In loving God, we obey God—and with good reason. Consider the following:

Learning Activity
The Three Witnesses

Read 1 John 5:6-8. In your opinion, how do we find Jesus fulfilling the role of these three witnesses? Record your responses in the space below.

• The Spirit:

• The Water:

• The Blood:

a. God's commandments are a blessing (5:2). His commandments are a blessing because they free us to live not as we *want*, but as we *ought*— indeed, as we should. Doing so brings us ultimate joy!

b. God's commandments are not a burden (5:3). God's commands aren't burdensome—a noun meaning heavy, crushing, and oppressive. Rather, they're a blessing (Matt 11:28-30). Love for God is demonstrated to be real only when we continually keep ("observe," "attend to carefully") His commandments. Love is not so much emotional as it is moral, not what you feel but what you do.

4. Christians experience victory by overcoming the world (5:4-5). God wants you to have victory in your Christian life by being an overcomer. In fact, four times John used this term, which is translated "victory," and means to conquer. Each of the letters to the seven churches in Revelation 2–3 ended with a challenge to be overcomers. But how is the Christian to "overcome?"

a. You must be born of God (5:4). This is the eighth time John addressed the new birth in this letter. Those who are of God will be conquerors over the world as a result of their faith. By being reborn through the death and resurrection of Christ, we defeat Satan, sin, and the evil system of this world. We defeat its idols, lies, greed, murder, racism, immorality, exploitation, and oppression. We defeat the heretics who oppose Christ and those who oppose all that is good.

b. You must believe in Jesus (5:5). Verse 5 is quite similar to verse 1, which declares that Jesus is the Christ. Verse 5 says Jesus is the Son of God. Thus John begins and ends with believing in Jesus. He set the foundation for victory over the world. It's only here that victory is won.

5. Christians experience victory by celebrating Jesus as God (5:6-10). Jesus was not only fully man; He was fully God too. Many things testify to His deity: His baptism, His death on the cross (5:6,8), the Holy Spirit (5:6,8), the Father Himself (5:9), and the believer's experience (by the indwelling Spirit).

Believing in Jesus as the Son of God is equivalent to accepting God's testimony about His Son (5:9). The result is that the Spirit testifies in the heart of the believer ("in himself"). It's a cause for celebration—God Himself is alive in you!

On the flip side, those who don't believe in Jesus are rejecting God's testimony and are essentially calling God a liar. Belief in the Father cannot be separated from belief in the Son.

6. Christians experience victory by celebrating eternal life (5:11-13). God has testified regarding His Son: eternal life is ours through His Son, Jesus Christ (5:11). This testimony leads into one of the most clearly stated verses in all of Scripture regarding the basic message of the Christian faith: "The one who has the Son has life. The one who doesn't have the Son of God does not have life." The terms "life" and "Son" are used five

times each in these verses. They fit together and can't be separated.

This testimony is the reason John wrote this letter, and verse 13 gives his fourth and greatest purpose statement (see also 1:4; 2:1; 2:26). John wanted his readers to *know with confidence* that they have eternal life. It's apparent that many in the church were being led astray by false teachings and made to doubt whether they possessed eternal life. However, God, who cannot lie, testifies that faith in His Son secures for us life with Him. This gives reason to celebrate our victory over death and sin!

In Christ Jesus we are more than conquerors in things both great and small. There's not one need He has not met by His death and resurrection. Our risen Lord has given us the victory!

For Your Consideration
1. What would you consider to be the overarching theme of 5:1-13?

2. What are some inevitable results of the new birth?

3. Why is obedience to God's commandments not burdensome for Christians?

4. List the reasons why so many people deny the deity of Jesus Christ. Is it because of a lack of convincing evidence or a refusal to accept the facts before them?

Faith's Confidence
(1 John 5:14-21)

The victory we experience as Christians has very practical application; it results in extraordinary confidence. Based on what God has said to us in 1 John 5:14-21, let us consider three areas where this confidence rests.

1. We are confident because God answers prayer (5:14-15). R. A. Torrey said, "All that God is and all that God has is at the disposal of prayer. But we must use the key. Prayer can do anything that God can do; and since God can do anything, prayer is omnipotent." Charles Spurgeon added, "Prayer moves the arm that moves the world."

John talked about prayer in 3:22. We're told that we can "receive whatever we ask from Him because we keep His commands and do what is pleasing in His sight." Now John once again addressed prayer, proclaiming that God

A CLOSER LOOK

Confidence

John has told us a number of things we can be confident of and know for sure:

1 John 2:3	We know God.
1 John 2:5	We are in Him.
1 John 3:14	We have passed from death to life.
1 John 4:18	We are loved by God.
1 John 5:3	We love God's children.
1 John 5:13	We have eternal life.
1 John 5:15	We have our prayers answered by God.
1 John 5:18	We don't live in sin.

hears our prayers when we pray according to His will. We must pray in two ways:

a. We pray confidently (2:28; 3:21; 4:17). We have boldness as we stand before our Father. We come as children to a loving Father who wants only what is best for us. When we pray, God hears us like a father listens to his children.

b. We pray carefully. Verse 14 again contains the crucial phrase "according to His will." Nothing we ask for lies beyond the power of God—except that which lies beyond His will and purpose. But why would you want something contrary to God's will? He *knows* and *wants* what's best—for His glory and our good. So, it's not only *right* to pray according to God's will; it is also *wise*.

2. We are confident because God restores those in sin (5:16-17). John was not soft on sin. In fact, the word "sin" or "sinning" occurs seven times in verses 16-18. It involves disobedience or a violation of God's moral standard. Sin is "missing the mark."

Because God hates sin, so should we. In fact, there should be a holy, righteous disgust in our hearts for the sin that captivates and dominates those enslaved by it. This is why John instructed us to pray for other believers who are caught in sin. Doing so is always in accordance with God's will. If we intercede for our brother or sister, God will hear us and grant life to the sinner. God strengthens and renews the life of the believer (3:14; 5:11-13).

All sin is serious, but not all sin leads to death. John's main concern was to encourage believers to pray for their brothers and sisters. In doing so, God often restores that person's relationship with Him.

1 cor 20:30

3. We are confident because Jesus keeps us from sin (5:18-21). In this letter, John spoke 10 times of the "new birth" in Christ. We call it "regeneration" or "conversion." John was not talking about our future glorified state. Rather, he was saying that Christ's transforming power results in a pure, "sinless" life *now*! Indeed, a Christian may stumble into sin, but he will not remain in sin. It will not be a habit of life. The reason the child of God does not continue in sin is because the Son of God "keeps him." Satan cannot put his hands on us because we rest safely in Christ's hands. He may attack us, but he cannot hold us. While sin and its consequences are to be taken seriously, the child of God is given power to overcome sin and to obey the will of God (see John 17:12; 1 Pet. 1:5; Jude 24). Thus, our security is not in ourselves, but in Jesus.

In 5:19-21, John related two truths concerning the effects of our "new birth" in Christ:

a. Jesus teaches us about our position with God (5:19). Where you stand spiritually is not only important, but also inescapable. There are only two options as to your position with God: either you're controlled by Satan and spiritually dead or you're a child of God and spiritually alive. John wrote that "the whole world is under the sway of the evil one," referring to society, culture, government, and earthly life. Satan controls the people of the world like a master controls a slave. They are trapped in sin and held there by Satan.

However, those rescued by Christ represent the second option for your position with God (John 12:31; John 14:30; John 16:11). They have an inner assurance in their souls that they belong to God. Knowing Jesus

A CLOSER LOOK

The Sin that Brings Death

The end of 1 John 5:16 is one of the most difficult verses in the Bible. Astonishingly, it tells us there is a sin for which no prayer will do any good. What is this "sin that brings death?" Three theories have been offered:

1. It could be a specific, deadly sin. Here it would be a willful and deliberate sin of a serious nature. Some see the "death" as physical, such as the death of Ananias and Sapphira (Acts 5:1-11), or the incestuous man at Corinth (1 Cor. 5:5), or the Corinthians abusing the Lord's Supper (1 Cor. 11:30).

2. It could be blasphemy against the Holy Spirit, such as that spoken about in Matthew 12:32 and Mark 3:29. It would be a deliberate, knowledgeable, willful, verbal, and continual rejection of the truth to which the Spirit bears witness. It is a hardening of the heart to a point that prayer will not help.

3. It could be a total rejection of the gospel and Christ, such as the sin of the false teachers who willfully and habitually oppose the witness of God in the person and work of His Son, Jesus Christ (see 2:19). This one is not called a brother. He is an apostate. In deliberately rejecting the Son of God who offers eternal life, they commit themselves to a spiritual attitude and course of action that could only be characterized as "sin unto death."

equals knowing God, and knowing God equals peace in your soul and certainty of your future (5:13).

b. Jesus also teaches us what to believe (5:20-21). We don't live in a world that believes *nothing*. Unfortunately, we live in a world that believes *everything*. What you believe and in whom you believe is crucial. False teachers always have subtracted or added to the doctrine of Jesus. If we misunderstand Jesus, we misunderstand God for "He is the true God and eternal life." Jesus has come and "has given us understanding so that we may know the true One." This understanding is related to our "new birth." Here is the sole foundation for the truth about God and genuine spiritual life. Stay with Jesus, and you'll be safe from error and deception. Stay with

Jesus, and you'll be safe from sin and Satan. Jesus is the true God and eternal life.

Beware, however, for there are false gods. That's why John ended his letter by warning his "children" to guard themselves from idols (5:21). So, while we are kept by Christ (v. 18), we must still be on guard against "God-substitutes." It is vital that we remain pure in our focus on God's glory (Col. 3:5).

Jesus Christ is the Son of God, the true God, the only God who provides eternal life to anyone who comes to Him in faith. He's the true revelation of God. Anything else is a counterfeit and a false substitute. On this truth, one can be certain. Here one can and should stake their eternal destiny. This is where John ends. This is where we should stand.

For Your Consideration:

1. If God asks you, "Why should I let you into my heaven?" what will you say? What do verses 16 and 17 teach that God will want to hear?

2. John wrote this letter so that his readers would experience four things:
   - absolute joy (1:4);
   - the absence of unconfessed sin (2:1);
   - protection from false teaching (2:26); and
   - assurance of eternal life (5:13).

Do these four things characterize your life? If not, ask God to help you work on those areas and to make them a daily reality.

Keep on Living in Truth and Love

BIBLE TRUTH: *Believers who consistently live in truth and love encourage others in their faith and service to God.*

LIFE IMPACT: *To help you live consistently in truth and love*

Show Love and Hold to the Truth
(2 John)

There is a clash of world views taking place in America today. Unfortunately, the Church appears to be losing the battle. Truth is an endangered species in our secular, relativistic culture. Likewise, love is in grave danger of devolving into nothing more than shallow sentimentalism because there are so many inferior imitations.

Because of America's present truth crisis, the letter of 2 John has words of insight that address the heart and mind—love and truth. Though it's the second shortest book of the Bible with only 245 words (3 John has 219 words), John delivered four words of instruction and encouragement for those who would be guardians of God's eternal truth.

John ("the Elder") had a personal and intimate relationship with his readers. He was an aged but respected man of moral standing and reputation. The recipient is identified as "the elect lady and her children," most likely a local church body. The phrase carries with it the notion of respect, endearment, and concern. God chose them. They belonged to Him, and He cared for them personally. He loved them, and God (through John) instructed them regarding the issue of truth.

1. We should love the truth (vv. 1-3). John expressed his love for this body of believers. He did so in the context of *truth*, a truth shared by all who know it. This truth continually abides *in* us and *with* us forever. Truth in the biblical sense is essential, not optional; eternal, not relative; consistent, not changing.

This truth flows from the One who is "the way, the truth and the life" (John 14:6) and who is Himself "the true God and eternal life" (1 John 5:20). John encouraged us to embrace this truth.

Furthermore, truth is accompanied by many blessings such as grace, mercy, and peace. *Grace* is God doing for us what we do not deserve (unmerited favor and kindness). *Mercy*, on the other hand, is God not doing to us what we do deserve. Finally, *peace* is personal wholeness and well-being in all aspects of life (see Rom. 5:1; Phil. 4:9). As seen in verse 3, these enjoyable blessings flow *equally* from God the Father and Jesus the Son.

2. We should live the truth (vv. 4-6). Key words such as walk, commandment(s), doctrine, deceivers, and antichrist drive John's argument in verses 4-11. In verses 4-6 we learn how to actually *live* the truth.

a. We should concern ourselves with what we believe (v. 4). John was overjoyed to find that this particular church was "walking in truth," just as they were commanded to do by the Father. This truth is spiritual, not philosophical, and rests on the authority of Jesus Christ. Tragically, many people today face a crisis of authority when it comes to truth. There are only four options as to what we may submit our beliefs and actions: reason ("I think it"), experience ("I feel it"), tradition ("We've always done it"), and revelation ("God says it"). God has

spoken and that settles the issue of authority. What God says is true, and we should obey Him.

b. We should also be concerned with our behavior (vv. 5-6). Truth is something we live, and it will always make a beeline to love. Since the beginning of our Christian experience, the commandment to love each other has been before us (see John 13:34-35). In fact, love flows naturally from the truth. Since John's readers were "walking in the truth" (v. 4), he was confident that they would welcome his call to love one another.

John said that walking in truth pleases God and that obeying His commandments demonstrate our love for Him. Verses 4–6 say it almost poetically: walk in the commandment to love, and love the commandments in which you walk. Truth is something we practice.

3. We should look for the truth (vv. 7-11). Truth is not always easy to find. Our postmodern society has declared that truth is *made* not *found*—that a text of Scripture has no fixed meaning. Rather, the meaning of any given text is simply constructed by its reader.

The apostle John said that where truth is twisted, heresy will reign. He fought for truth when he confronted the heresy of Gnosticism. Gnosticism (meaning "knowledge") developed into many forms, but one common thread was their unrelenting attack on the incarnation (God becoming man).

John knew that Christology is the heart of Christianity, and he issued a strong warning to be on the lookout for anyone who challenges the full deity, perfect humanity, sinless life, and completed work of Jesus Christ. It's important to both recognize and reject deceptive teaching.

John called these false teachers "deceivers" and "antichrists," meaning that such false teaching is "against Christ. John warned us that we should continually be on guard and resist those who deny the truth about Jesus and who would take from us our full reward (see 1 John 2:19; 2 Cor. 13:5).

Spiritual destroyers will deny:
- the truthfulness and sufficiency of the Bible;
- the person and work of Jesus Christ—His full deity and/or perfect humanity, along with His work of atonement on the cross as the perfect sacrifice for our sin;
- His sinless life, virgin birth, bodily resurrection, and historical coming again in glory; and
- salvation as a free gift received by grace through faith in Christ alone.

According to verse 9, false teachers twist the truth by "going beyond it." They leave the basic biblical truths about Jesus while claiming to offer

A CLOSER LOOK

The Mathematics of the Cults

Addition	They add an extra-biblical source of authority by prophet, pen, or professor.
Subtraction	They subtract from the person and work of Jesus Christ by denying His deity and finding inadequate His work of redemption.
Division	They divide our allegiance from God through Christ alone to others.
Multiplication	They multiply requirements for salvation by advocating some form of works salvation.

something new and better. We see this today with such groups as the Mormons, Jehovah's Witnesses, New Age groups, Spiritualists, and others. Without exception, all false teachers practice a very similar mathematical strategy.

Whenever someone adds to the biblical testimony of Jesus, a subtraction from the truth is inevitable. John's judgment was quick and to the point: such persons are lost. They do not have God. Because they are not from God, John tells us that they and their teaching must be rejected (vv. 10-11). We should not assist these false teachers in their evil works because, if we do, we're accomplices in spreading heresy (3 John 8). John was not being unloving or unkind; rather, he was simply being pastoral and practical. We cannot pray God's blessings on those who deny our Lord and reject the teachings of God's Word.

So how should we act toward someone involved in a cult? First, always be kind, be a good listener, pray for them, and love them. Second, follow a four-step proce-dure: (1) Ask them to tell you how they believe salvation is obtained, and give them 15 uninterrupted minutes; (2) Require that they give you 15 minutes uninterrupted so that you can tell them how you believe a person can be saved and go to heaven; (3) Pray with them, and pray evangelistically, clearly sharing the gospel in your prayer; and (4) Invite them (and their friends) back to do it again!

Throughout his epistles, John stressed love. However, he didn't stress love to the point that truth is twisted and false teaching is accommodated. We must be on the look-out for truth, and we will recognize the truth by what it says about Jesus Christ.

4. *We should long for the truth (vv. 12-13).* John had shared his heart, but there was much more he wanted to say. Paper and pen had been sufficient for the immediate situation, but they were a poor substitute for a "face to face" meeting. In closing, John reminded his readers of two precious truths never to be taken for granted.

a. We should experience the fullness of joy (v. 12). The phrase "face to face" is a beautiful Greek idiom which literally translates "mouth to mouth." When believers who love the Lord Jesus and each other come together, there is indeed a fullness of joy which words cannot express.

b. We should experience the fellowship of the family (v. 13). The letter closed with a greeting from a sister church which stood with John in what he had written. The truth about Jesus brings together believers from every tribe, people, tongue, and nation. We are one big family with the same Father, Savior, and Spirit.

Jesus Christ defines both history and eternity. Truth does exist—and it matters. We must love the truth and live the truth. Jesus said, "You shall know the truth and the truth shall make you free" (John 8:32).

For Your Consideration
1. What gave John such great joy? Why?

2. What are some characteristics of false teaching?

Learning Activity

Long for the Truth
(2 John 12-13)

Read 2 John 12-13 and answer the questions below.
Work with a partner to complete this exercise.

1. How does this passage express the fullness of joy
   in the life of the believer?

2. How does this passage express the fellowship of
   the family in the life of the church?

3. How would you respond to the above questions in
   relation to your own life?

3. How does welcoming false teaching contribute to wickedness?

4. How can we avoid false teaching without being cold or inhospitable?

Work with Others Who Teach in Truth and Love
(3 John)

Our reputation accompanies us wherever we go. Good or bad, it also goes where we don't go. Whether our reputations are good or bad, we can be assured of this: (1) we all have a reputation; (2) people will watch us and talk about us; and (3) we cannot escape or lose our reputation. It precedes us, goes with us, and follows us all of our lives and beyond.

Like 1 and 2 Timothy, Titus, Philemon (and possibly 2 John), 3 John was written to an individual, a man named Gaius. While 2 John is concerned with *truth*, 3 John is primarily concerned with *love*. The outline of 3 John focuses on the four men in the letter.

Gaius: A Commendable Christian (vv. 1-8)

Four times in this letter John addressed Gaius as "beloved" or "dear friend." John also addressed four praiseworthy areas of Gaius' life. Like Gaius, we should seek to excel in these areas of life.

1. We should live spiritually (vv. 1-2). Although Gaius may have been suffering some physical difficulty, his spiritual life was given a clean bill of health. Gaius was "soul healthy."

2. We should walk truthfully (vv. 3-4). This is intimately connected with living spiritually. John could rejoice greatly because of what others were telling him about Gaius. The truth was in him, and he acted accordingly. In doctrine and deed, we should be commendable, praiseworthy, and a joy to others.

People can't see your heart, but they can see your life.

3. We should serve faithfully (vv. 5-6). Love is an action word! Gaius was showing hospitality and entertaining both brothers and strangers alike. John encouraged Gaius to continue what he was doing (providing lodging, food, money, and encouragement to God's servants).

4. We should minister generously (vv. 7-8). Though most of us are not full-time missionaries in the strictest sense, we share in missionaries' calling as their partners. Senders, who generously support those who go, are essential as we cooperate together in the work of God.

There is no limit to how much good you can do if you do not care who gets the credit. Gaius was a commendable Christian.

Diotrephes: A Conceited Christian (vv. 9-10)

Diotrephes was far from a commendable Christian. He may not have even been a Christian. He wanted to be the "boss" in the church, and he opposed the apostle John with perverted ambition and a dominating spirit. If anyone objected to him, that person was censured and dismissed from the congregation. Unfortunately, many people in the church today mirror Diotrephes' lust for power. John condemned Diotrephes in several areas.

1. Avoid prideful ambition and pompous arrogance (vv. 9-10). John wrote a letter now lost to us, and Diotrephes objected to its contents. His objection was not about doctrine but personal pride. He loved being "the top dog" and the center of attention. Such a position is reserved for Jesus alone (Col. 1:18). Incredibly, he felt the apostle had nothing to offer, nothing he needed! Such arrogance would have been culturally shameful. It's spiritually unbelievable.

Tragically, many today attempt to take for themselves the position reserved for Jesus alone. While we don't know who Diotrephes was, we do know he was driven by prideful ambition and arrogance.

Learning Activity
Quality Control

Scan 3 John. Record below the characteristics of each individual who is listed and how your life resembles theirs.

Individual	Characteristics of the Individual	How does my life resemble this individual?
Gaius (vv. 1-8)		
Diotrephes (vv 9-10)		
Demetrius (vv. 11-12)		
John (vv. 13-15)		

2. Avoid perverse accusations and profane activity (v. 10). Diotrephes was slandering John with malicious words. John said that when he came to town, he would confront Diotrephes' destructive behavior (1 Tim. 5:20).

There's a sad digression to Diotrephes' behavior: ambition led to arrogance, which led to accusations, which ended with action. He acted exactly the opposite of Gaius.

Demetrius: A Consistent Christian (vv 11-12)

John knew that we tend to imitate others. We must be careful whom we look up to. Demetrius is an exemplary man worthy of our admiration.

Like Demetrius, we should pursue godly examples (v. 11). Ultimately, we should imitate Jesus. However, we need earthly examples to imitate as well.

John wrote, "Do not imitate [or mimic] what is evil, but what is good" because whom we imitate gives evidence of to whom we belong! So be careful who you watch, and be mindful of who's watching you!

Furthermore, like Demetrius, we should possess a good testimony (v. 12). Interestingly, it was probably Demetrius who brought this letter to Gaius. John said in verse 12 that three different "witnesses" testify to Demetrius' godliness: (1) everyone around him; (2) the truth itself; and (3) John and the people in his community.

While it's doubtful that everyone in his town agreed with Demetrius' Christian beliefs, no one could question his character. Everyone was amazed at his integrity and godliness. He walked with God. Here was a man people could point out to their children and say, "Be like him." Could people also say that about you?

John: A Caring Christian (vv. 13-14)

Through positive and negative examples, John painted a portrait of good, godly leadership. His closing thoughts should guide our attitude toward our brothers and sisters in the faith.

Like John, we should desire the presence of fellow believers. With a full and burdened heart, John longed to see them.

We should also desire peace for fellow believers. Christian brotherhood is amazing in that its love can be transmitted from miles away, and the believers in John's town were sending their love to Gaius. Interestingly, this is the only place in the New Testament that believers are called friends, perhaps reflecting John 15:13, where Jesus said, "No one has greater love than this, that someone would lay down his life for his friends."

Godly leadership is vital to a healthy church. James 4:6 reminds us that God resists the proud, but gives grace to the humble. Humility is the way of service. Humility is the way of spiritual greatness (Mark 10:35-45).

A CLOSER LOOK

Leadership is ...

Making wise decisions
Influencing friends to do what is right

Discerning people's hearts
Confidence
Hearing the voice of God
Being firm
Caring
Waiting on God
Hearing wise counsel

Leadership is not ...

Making snap decisions
Manipulating friends to do
 what we want
Judging other people harshly
Cockiness
Speaking in God's place
Being stubborn
Controlling
Procrastinating
Listening to anyone with an
 opinion

For Your Consideration
1. What does it mean to love someone in the truth?

2. What do you think of yourself?

3. What do you believe others think about you?

4. What does God think about you?

5. What would happen if someone were to pray and ask that God bless you physically to the degree that you are healthy spiritually? Would you be fit, in bed, or nearly dead? Would you be ready for a marathon or rushed to the emergency room?

CHRISTIAN GROWTH STUDY PLAN

In the **Christian Growth Study Plan (formerly Church Study Course),** this book, *John's Letters: How to Grow in Loving God,* is a resource for course credit in the subject area Leadership and Skill Development of the Christian Growth category of plans. To receive credit, read the book, complete the learning activities, show your work to your pastor, a staff member or church leader, then complete the following information. This page may be duplicated. Send the completed page to: **Christian**

Growth Study Plan • One LifeWay Plaza • Nashville, TN 37234-0117 • FAX: (615)251-5067 • Email: *cgspnet@lifeway.com.*

For information about the Christian Growth Study Plan, refer to the Christian Growth Study Plan Catalog. It is located online at *www.lifeway.com/cgsp*. If you do not have access to the Internet, contact the Christian Growth Study Plan office (1.800.968.5519) for the specific plan you need for your ministry.

John's Letters: How to Grow in Loving God
COURSE NUMBER: CG-1176

PARTICIPANT INFORMATION

Social Security Number (USA ONLY-optional) — —

Personal CGSP Number* —

Date of Birth (MONTH, DAY, YEAR) — —

Name (First, Middle, Last)

Home Phone —

Address (Street, Route, or P.O. Box)

City, State, or Province

Zip/Postal Code

Email Address for CGSP use

Please check appropriate box: ❑ Resource purchased by church ❑ Resource purchased by self ❑ Other

CHURCH INFORMATION

Church Name

Address (Street, Route, or P.O. Box)

City, State, or Province

Zip/Postal Code

CHANGE REQUEST ONLY

☐ Former Name

☐ Former Address

City, State, or Province

Zip/Postal Code

☐ Former Church

City, State, or Province

Zip/Postal Code

Signature of Pastor, Conference Leader, or Other Church Leader

Date

*New participants are requested but not required to give SS# and date of birth. Existing participants, please give CGSP# when using SS# for the first time. Thereafter, only one ID# is required. **Mail to:** Christian Growth Study Plan, One LifeWay Plaza, Nashville, TN 37234-0117. Fax: (615)251-5067.

Revised 4-05